PASTA, MEATBALLS, AND APPLE PIE

Our Son, John, a Love Story

D1428132

Evelyn Fraterrigo Artale

ISBN 978-1-64569-478-6 (paperback)
ISBN 978-1-64569-479-3 (digital)

Christian Faith Publishing, Inc.
832 Park Avenue
Meadville, PA 16335
www.christianfaithpublishing.com

Printed in the United States of America

PREFACE

I thought about writing this book several years ago. I knew the beginning of the story, what I wanted people to know about our son, John, who had learning disabilities, and what our life was like raising him. But I didn't have an ending and couldn't even think of one. However, John passed away on September 13, 2011, and now that I have an ending, I can begin to write. Over the years of John's life, I kept doctor's reports and most of the correspondence from different people and agencies involved with him. I'm glad that I did because relying only on my memories would never have been enough.

I dedicate this book to John's memory and to all of the people who were a part of his life through the years. It includes my husband, whose name is also John, our daughter Regina, some of our relatives and friends who offered prayers and support, but most of all, to those people who took care of John from age ten to the time he passed away. There were many of them—some good and some not-so good. Some of their names have been changed and some haven't. You'll meet them all (at least as many as I can remember). Know that I write this book with love and with the hope that it will help someone who faces a similar situation.

ACKNOWLEDGMENTS

We wouldn't have been able to endure the trials we had to go through and the many heartaches we would suffer without a great deal of prayer, our trust in God, and the support and encouragement of others.

First of all, my husband, John, took over many of my chores so that I would have more time to write. He also helped me to remember some of the things which I had forgotten. Robert who was a manager at Coachman, and Ted who became a real help when John was a resident at Woodbine, both took their time to come and visit us and share their remembrances of John. Barbara, a friend who read the book as I was writing it, became my personal cheerleader. She could hardly wait until the next chapter was done. Rocco who gave me tips on how to best use my computer for writing this book. Then there were the many relatives, friends, and neighbors who prayed for me all along the way. Finally, without the guidance of the Holy Spirit, this book would never have been written.

CHAPTER

1

Before I introduce you to our son, John, I think it's important for you to know a little about me and my husband. I was born and brought up in the Bronx, New York. Funny, none of the other boroughs of New York City have *the* before their name, only "the Bronx". My mom was a dressmaker and my dad a custom tailor. I grew up with two older brothers, one passed away several years ago. None of this is relevant to the story, but what is relevant is that I had no sister which I always wished that I had. I thought of us as being a small family, so I thought about having lots of children when I got married. As you'll see, that didn't happen.

Also growing up, I loved to sing and act and dreamed that some-day, I would have a stage career. That too didn't happen. My parents didn't think that having a family and a career could go together and because I was a good daughter, I obeyed them and never pursued the career I had dreamed about. I wasn't very happy about it, and I became very resentful and angry until I realized that God had a different plan for my life—a very different plan—one that turned out to be the best plan for me.

My husband was born and brought up in Brooklyn, New York. Not "the Brooklyn," just plain Brooklyn. John was an only child. His mother wasn't well, and she died of cancer when he was a teenager. His father remarried shortly after, but nevertheless, there were no other siblings. John never gave much thought about what he wanted to do with his life until high school. He decided then that he wanted to be an engineer. He graduated from college with a degree in civil engineering. At age twenty-three, John entered the navy and after three years of service, he was discharged as a lieutenant. It was during his last year in the navy that we met.

CHAPTER 2

One of my cousins, who happened to be a fraternity brother of my husband, introduced us. John thought it was time for him to settle down, and he was interested in meeting someone with whom he hoped to get serious. It was in June 1955, when he was home for a weekend, that he telephoned my cousin, Ron, and asked if he or his wife, Lee, knew of anyone who might be interested in meeting him. Ron thought of me and told John that he would look into it.

Ron phoned me and asked if I would like to meet a friend of his. Of course, he would have to get my father's permission before he could introduce us. That's the way it was done in our family. Ron told us that he knew John from college, that he was a fine young man, that he was an officer in the navy, and that he was Italian. Back in those days, same ethnic origin was a plus in any relationship that could possibly lead to marriage. It certainly was a big hit with my dad and mom and many of my relatives when they met him. The same was true for John's family when they met me.

We hit it off well and found out that we had a lot in common especially our love for opera and good Italian food. Luckily I had learned to cook from an early age and had lots of experience at it. Over the sixty-plus years of our marriage, about 99 percent of my cooking was Italian food. The other 1 percent included French, German, Polish, Russian, Jewish, Hawaiian, and Chinese. I told you, I liked to cook, and we both liked to eat. As far as my husband was concerned, no one made spaghetti and meatballs better than me. To this day, he compares it to any other that he eats.

Somewhere in our courtship, we fell in love and were married a year and a half after we met. One of the things we both very much agreed on was that we wanted to have a big family of our own. We thought that six children would be our goal. That didn't happen. Once again, God had a different plan. His plan was one we could never have imagined or dreamed of. Yet looking back, we know that it was the best plan for both of us.

CHAPTER 3

During the first few weeks of our marriage, since we both looked forward to having a large family, I thought for sure that I would become pregnant. We were young and in good health. My husband had a good job with good pay. To our disappointment, however, that didn't happen either. About a year after we were married, John changed jobs and went to work in Paterson, New Jersey. He had to commute from our apartment in Riverdale, New York every day and after a year of doing that, we decided to buy a house in New Jersey. We found the perfect one for us in the town of Fair Lawn.

The months kept going by, and I still wasn't pregnant. We finally came to the conclusion that something must be wrong. So we consulted our doctor who recommended that we see a specialist who would know more than he did about our problem. We decided to follow his advice, got in touch with a specialist and made an appointment to see him. There was an initial consultation followed by examinations and a couple of tests. His conclusion was that we each had a problem which, put together, would never enable us to conceive our own children. Wow! What a blow! What do we do now?

It took some time for the reality of the situation to sink in. We thought about adoption and discussed the pros and cons many times. Then we finally decided that our family would be just as wonderful and complete with adopted children. There was no reason why we couldn't give our love to them just as if they had been born to us. So we started the process by making a phone call to the Catholic Charities Adoption Agency in Newark, New Jersey. We were connected to Ms. Laura Nielson, one of the principal social workers at Catholic Charities, and we made an appointment to go in to see her for an interview.

CHAPTER 4

M s. Nielson was very pleasant and very professional. She asked us many questions, starting with why do we want to adopt a child? This was followed by did we want a boy or a girl? Would it matter if the child was from another country? Would it matter if the child wasn't an infant? None of these mattered to us. We would accept any child and give it our love. She asked us about our ethnic background, and what were our likes and dislikes? Were we financially stable? Could we afford to raise a child? Ms. Nielson then informed us that the child would need to have its own room, that we would need a letter from the doctor with his diagnosis regarding the fact that we weren't able to conceive our own children, reference letters from our pastor regarding our status in the church, a letter from my husband's current employer, a statement from our bank showing our account record, and reference letters from three other people who were not immediate family. The letters were to go directly to her. We had no trouble with any of this.

Ms. Nielson advised us that the adoption process would take some time and that we wouldn't even be considered as adoptive parents until we were marred for five years which meant that we'd have two more years to go. Another blow! Weren't there any babies out there just waiting to be adopted? It seemed absurd; but then again, I guess that they wanted couples who would still be married after living together for five years and had faced the many issues which couples struggle with in those first years. Back then, we didn't know any couples who lived together before marriage, and we realized that it takes at least that long to get to really know each other as only married couples do. Our faults, our shortcomings and annoying habits, have a way of showing up during those first years. In-law problems and money problems can also become unpleasant issues for some newlyweds.

We agreed to all of the requirements, accepted the application, took a deep breath, and went home to think about what we just went through, and then started asking for the necessary letters. We were confident that we could go through all of this with flying colors. We did, and now we would just have to wait for the right time and the right child.

CHAPTER
5

The time seemed to crawl by. Then I think it was in January of 1961, we got a phone call from Ms. Nielson saying that she would like us to make an appointment to go in to see her. Since the five-year waiting period wouldn't be up until September, we thought that she wanted to let us know whether the letters of reference had arrived and whether or not they were to her satisfaction. However, when we got there, much to our surprise, she told us that she had located a child whom she thought we might be interested in. I could hardly believe my ears! Did I really hear her say what I thought she said? I was so overwhelmed with emotions that I could hardly speak. If I could speak, I wouldn't have known what to say. I didn't know whether to laugh, cry, or shout, "Hallelujah!" Then she took out a photo of him and handed it to me.

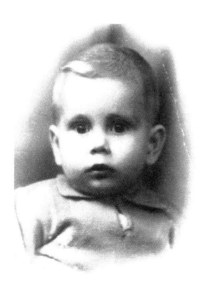

Our first photo of John.

When I saw his picture, I immediately fell in love with him. He had dark-blond hair and the most beautiful, biggest, dark-brown eyes I had ever seen, but they also looked sad. They looked straight at me and said, "Please take me home." Ms. Nielson then asked us if we would consider adopting him even though he was almost three years old. Was she kidding? We were married almost five years, and he was almost three years old. It was perfect!

Ms. Nielson then went on to tell us that the child was brought to an orphanage in Aquila, Italy, and left there by a woman who said that she was his grandmother, although they weren't sure about that. She also told us that his birth mother was a young, unmarried girl and that there wasn't anything noted about his birth father.

After that, Ms. Nielson went on to tell us that the orphanage, where our soon-to-be son lived, was very poor and understaffed. The children there were limited in what they had to eat so for the most part, they were undernourished. Also because they were understaffed and the children weren't able to get the attention they needed, she told us that Mario, the name which was given to our son by the registrar of births in Italy, had never spoken, he was not toilet-trained, and was very withdrawn. No wonder he looked so sad! She also said that he was a child who needed lots of love and care and that in time, he would be fine. We certainly were ready, willing, and able to give him all of the love that he needed, and we agreed to go ahead with the adoption. It would take three months before all of the necessary paperwork would be completed, and the first thing we had to do was to apply for a visa.

CHAPTER

6

We told all of our relatives and friends the good news that finally, we were going to become mama and papa to a little boy from Italy. Needless to say, everyone was very happy for us. Our friends threw us a surprise party, and what a great party it was. Besides all of the gifts and good food, Vinnie, who was always the more or less quiet one, dressed up like a little Italian boy, wearing short pants, a round straw-hat and a string bow tie, and came skipping in with arms opened wide, calling out, "Mama! Papa!" That made the party even more special. Then on April 12, we got the long-awaited phone call. We were instructed by Ms. Nielson to go to a hotel in downtown New York City the next evening where we would meet a social worker and pick up our son. It was the happiest phone call we had ever gotten. April 13, 1961, was to be the big day which we had waited so long for, and it couldn't come fast enough!

CHAPTER 7

It was finally time for us to venture in to New York City. We had no trouble finding the hotel even though it was one which we had never heard of before, and we were lucky enough to find a parking space not too far from the entrance to the hotel. We were greeted by a social worker, Lea Dante, who introduced herself and asked us for identification which included a letter from Catholic Charities. We quickly gave it to her. After she looked it over and gave it back, she said that she would go and get Mario and bring him down to us. My husband, John, and I looked at each other and tightly held our hands together. This was it. Finally!

When Lea came out of the elevator holding our son, I could see that he had on a tan spring coat with a matching cap, brown shoes, and short pants. He was sound asleep. He must've been very heavy for her because she plopped him into my arms like a sack of potatoes. Looking at his beautiful face, tears welled up in my eyes. Then my eyes worked their way down to his bare legs, and I saw several scabs, some of which were quite large, on the sides of both his legs. When I asked what they were, Lea said that she didn't know. My husband then had to read and sign a paper which said that Mario had arrived safely and was now in our care. That was it, and we left. It would take a year before the adoption would become final, and the time started now.

The ride home was rather quiet except that we talked about what had just taken place and that it was rather cold. Lea had a job to do, and she did it without any emotion at all on her part. I guess with that kind of job, there isn't much room for emotions. We also agreed that the next day, we would take our son, John, who would be named after his dad and who from now on, would be known as

Johnny (obviously to distinguish between him and my husband), to a doctor to find out what the scabs were all about. Johnny slept all the way home.

CHAPTER 8

When we finally arrived home, we were greeted by our little black dog, Cindy. She was wagging her tail, barking because she was happy to see us, and jumping up and down, trying to see what in the world I was carrying. We brought Johnny into our bedroom and put him down on the bed. Immediately Cindy jumped up onto the bed and began to sniff Johnny which woke him up. He looked a little frightened at first. He looked at us, and then he looked at Cindy and started to laugh. I don't think that he had ever seen a dog before especially one that jumped around and sniffed him.

Cindy was given to us by my brother, Rudy, because she had become jealous of their baby, Cathy, and would growl at her. Now Cathy was grown up, and Cindy soon became jealous of Johnny, so we asked my brother to take her back. We had to say goodbye to Cindy. We knew that we'd miss her but unfortunately, she had to go.

Luckily John and I both spoke some Italian. We explained to Johnny, as best that we could, where he was and who we were. I held him as we spoke, told him that we loved him and that we were his mama and papa. He just stared at us with his big, beautiful eyes. I then took off his clothes and put him into pajamas that had long sleeves and long pants with foot covers. I figured that would keep him from scratching his legs. When we took off his clothes, we were somewhat shocked. We could see that not only were his arms and legs very thin but that he also had a distended belly just like the children you see on TV who are starving in Africa. Ms. Nielson wasn't kidding when she told us that the orphanage in Aquila was very poor and that the children were undernourished. I wonder if she had any idea just how malnourished the children there really were, and I prayed that things would get better for them. I finally got Johnny into his own bed, which was in the room right next to ours, and stayed with him until he fell asleep. As I sat there with him, I gently ran my hand over his hair and softly sang to him. Little did I know that this would become one of Johnny's favorite things.

CHAPTER
9

I got up a couple of times during the night to make sure that Johnny was all right, but the next morning when we went to wake him, Johnny wasn't in his bed. We thought that he probably got out of bed and went looking around the house, but he wasn't in any of the other rooms. Where in the world did he go? Just when we were asking ourselves that, we heard a sound coming from under his bed. Sure enough, there he was. We didn't know how he got under there or why he was under there. Had he fallen out and couldn't get back into bed? Was he frightened and tried to hide? Could it be that he wasn't used to sleeping in a bed?

Whatever the reason, my husband got him out. Johnny did look a little frightened, so I held him close and tried to tell him, as best as I could in Italian, that he was a good boy, that we loved him, and that he should sleep in his bed and not under it. We went out that day and bought a guardrail to make sure that he wouldn't fall out of bed again. It went only halfway down so that he wouldn't feel trapped. He never slept under the bed again. For some reason, however, he seemed to prefer sleeping on the floor, and it took a while before he slept in his bed through the night.

I don't remember what I gave him to eat for breakfast that first day, but I did remember that Ms. Nielson told us that he didn't know how to use a spoon. However, whatever it was that we gave him to eat, Johnny devoured it as quickly as he could, using his little fingers. I tried feeding him, but I wasn't fast enough. He ate a second helping in the same way. We realized that he was probably eating like that because he wasn't sure when the next meal would be coming. After that first meal, we put a limit on what he ate, making sure that he had enough, and taught him how to eat with a spoon. It didn't take more than a couple of days for Johnny to know that enough food would be coming to him every day. He ate everything that was put in front of him and liked it all. It took only a couple more days before he learned to use a spoon. The next thing we did that day was to get an appointment with the doctor. In anticipation of our adopting a child, I asked some of our friends with children for the name of their pediatrician. Almost everyone we asked recommended Dr. M. Roberts who was a pediatric neurologist.

I called the doctor's office and explained to the receptionist that we were in the process of adopting this little boy who had just come over from Italy, that he had scabs on his legs which we knew nothing about, that he looked malnourished, and that it was urgent for us to bring him in to see the doctor as soon as possible. We got an appointment for that afternoon. Johnny didn't speak, but we would always tell him what was happening, where we were going and why, reassuring him that he was a good boy, that we loved him, and that everything was alright. He didn't have to be afraid.

We got to meet Dr. Roberts and explained that we were in the process of adopting Johnny and that when we picked him up the night before, we saw the scabs on his legs but the social worker didn't know what they were. He was appalled. After examining Johnny, he told us that the scabs were a secondary infection from chicken pox, that we should keep them covered and free from being scratched, and he gave us a prescription to help get rid of them. What he told us next, however, was something that no parent wants to hear. Dr. Roberts said that Johnny was neurologically impaired and that he would never be normal. He advised us to give him back and that if we didn't, we would be facing a very difficult life. My immediate response was, "If I had given birth to this child, could I give him back?" We left the office with aching hearts, but we knew right from that moment that God put this little boy from Italy in our care for a reason and that no matter what, he was ours to keep and to love. We also knew that we would do everything possible to find out just how neurologically impaired Johnny was and what, if anything, we could do for him. Little did we know that Dr. Roberts, besides being a good doctor, was also a prophet.

CHAPTER

10

We didn't expect to hear the bad news about Johnny's condition. We were taken by surprise and were shocked when Dr. Roberts' words reached our ears. We found it hard to believe. The agency made no mention of it except that he was far behind in his development. Neurological impairment was not noted anywhere in his medical records, and the fact that he was so far behind in his development as a two, almost three-year-old might have been a normal-like condition in the orphanage, so they probably didn't think much about it. Most likely, they were grateful that he was so quiet and didn't cry for their attention.

Now, however, we certainly had a lot of questions to ask ourselves. How was this going to affect our lives? Would we be able to handle it? What were our dreams for our son, and what would his future be like instead? Would we have the courage, the compassion, the inner struggle to walk with him on the journey he'd have to take throughout his whole life? Would our love for him be enough? There would also be times when we would question God like why did He allow this to happen to us? And lastly, how in the world were we going to break the news to our parents, family, and friends? The only way we could answer these questions was to move forward with our lives one day at a time, trusting that God would be there to help us and to show us the way no matter what the future would be like for Johnny or for us. We would most likely have to make some life-changing decisions. Not only did we ourselves have to pray for guidance, but we also needed to rely on others who were prayerful, wise, objective, compassionate, caring, and willing to travel this road with us. We found them in our loving family and friends. We were moving into unknown territory, and we had no way of knowing how difficult it would be.

Facing the unknown can be scary. No one can accurately predict the future, but we knew that there would be times when we would feel stress, sorrow, fear, doubt, guilt, anger, confusion, worry, and at a loss for words. We also knew, without a doubt, that we would help this beautiful child, our son, to grow, to learn, and to give him all of the love and the security which he needed and would continue to need as he grew up. What we could never have imagined, however, was how much we would learn about ourselves, about our capacity to love, and about how much we would be blessed because we said yes and accepted this beautiful little boy from Italy into our lives and into our hearts.

CHAPTER 11

Over the next few weeks, we spent a lot of time helping Johnny with his adjustment to a new life. Besides a new name, a new home, and a whole new environment, he had to learn a new language. We decided after struggling with speaking to Johnny in Italian that it was time to speak to him in English and see how it would go. At first, we would say words to him in Italian and translate them to English. After doing that for a while, we dropped the Italian and spoke to him only in English. Much to our surprise, he responded rather quickly to the new language and seemed to be able to adjust in a short time to his whole new life.

However, there was an incident which happened before the change in language. One afternoon, Johnny and I were sitting at our kitchen table. I don't recall what happened. Whether something spilled or broke, I'm not sure but whatever it was, Johnny became very frightened. He quickly got down from his chair, went over to the wall, and put both his hands behind him. His eyes were full of fear. I knelt down in front of him, put out my hand, and said in Italian, "Dammi la mano (give me your hand)." He pushed himself against the wall even harder, so I reached behind him and grabbed his hand, forced it out from behind him, and brought it up to my lips and kissed it. He pulled his hand away and put it behind him again. Once more, I said, "Dammi la mano," and again, I had to reach back and force it out. This time, there was a little less resistance. Nevertheless, when I kissed his little hand again, he pulled it away and back it went behind him. I'm sure that he didn't know what was happening. I tried a third time and waited to see what he would do. I repeated, "Dammi la mano," once or twice, and then fear seemed to disappear from his eyes. Very cautiously, he took his hand out from behind him, gave it to me, and let me put it up to my lips to kiss it. I hugged him and told him that he was a good boy, that I loved him and would never hurt him. It was a beautiful moment which I'll never forget. It was the moment when Johnny knew that he could trust me.

CHAPTER 12

One of the first things I had to do was to get Johnny toilet-trained. Back then, there were no Pampers. Diapers were square linen cloths which had to be washed and reused, folded a certain way, and pinned with four safety pins especially made for that purpose. Two of the pins were fastened to a tab on each side of an undershirt. There were paper diaper liners which didn't really help all that much and a plastic panty to put over the diaper to keep things from getting wet. It wasn't a very pleasant thing to do especially since Johnny was almost three years old and didn't like wearing diapers any more than I liked changing them. I think that the little children at the orphanage probably didn't wear any undergarments at all. I don't know how, but the nuns must've found another way to handle it. Anyhow the task at hand took top priority. I don't remember how long it took, but it wasn't too long before the problem was resolved. Johnny learned to use the toilet and to indicate to us when he had to go.

The next few months were all about learning to play. One thing I noticed was that Johnny didn't play with his toys. Sometimes he'd pick them up, look at them, and then put them down again. He didn't know what they were or what to do with them. Then I realized that he probably didn't have anything much to play with as an infant. So I sat down on the floor and rolled a ball to him. He didn't roll it back. Then I showed him what to do and tried again just like you would with an infant who never before played with a ball. After a couple more tries, he learned to do it. It was the same with all of his toys. Cars, trucks, blocks, push toys, pull toys—they were all new to him. One by one, he learned to play with and enjoy his toys.

Johnny also loved to bang on my pots with a wooden spoon and enjoyed putting a paper shopping bag over his head and walking around until he came to a wall, then he'd laugh, turn around, and walk the other way. At first, I didn't like that idea; but I watched him, and he always seemed to know when to stop and which way to turn and walk away. It was his own little game. He never got hurt and was never more than a few feet away from me, so I let him have fun until he got tired of it which wasn't very long.

Another thing Johnny liked to do was to wind the end of his shirt around his finger. He'd wind and unwind over and over again. I decided to tie a string to a spoon and showed him how to wind and unwind it. He must've thought that it was a good idea because before long, wherever Johnny went, the spoon and string went with him.

Johnny and I enjoyed playing outside in the backyard and going for little walks to visit some of our neighbors. Josie always had chocolate candy for him, and Pat had a children's-size carousel in her backyard which Johnny enjoyed riding on. Barbara was a newlywed and didn't have children yet, and she enjoyed playing with Johnny. Abe and Helen were retired and loved to make a fuss over him which he thoroughly enjoyed. The best thing about it was that Johnny, even though he didn't talk, he'd always have a big beautiful smile on his face whenever we visited our neighbors. All in all, teaching Johnny to play and watching him laugh was fun for both of us.

Before moving on with my story, there's one more thing to tell you. Every night around 6:15, Johnny and I would drive to the train station in town to meet Daddy when he came home from work. I explained to him where we were going and why and that he would see a very big train. Of course, he didn't know what a big train was so when he heard the whistle and saw the train for the first time, he was frightened. I picked him up and held him tight. Then when he saw Daddy, he was happy. There were hugs and kisses, and Daddy carried Johnny to the car. We went home for supper. After that first time, Johnny looked forward to seeing the train and meeting Daddy at the station. Whenever he heard the train whistle blow, he got very excited and even learned to wave to the conductor who looked for us every night. It was a special time of day for the three of us.

CHAPTER

13

A word about grandparents. My husband, John, and I have seven grandchildren. Being grandparents ourselves, we know that having grandchildren is a gift from God. Everyone I know has "the best grandchildren in the world," and they are all special in their own way. It was the same for our parents when they first met Johnny.

John's mom and dad lived in Brooklyn and even though Dad drove, New Jersey wasn't exactly around the corner. I'm sure that they wished we lived closer. Because my husband had no siblings, his parents weren't used to dealing with little children; however, they took to Johnny right away. Both of them still worked, so they came to visit only on weekends whenever they could and enjoyed their visits with us. Especially Dad who liked to play with Johnny.

My mom and dad lived in the Bronx. Neither one of them drove. They had to take the subway to the George Washington Bridge bus terminal and then take another bus which brought them to Fair Lawn. John had to pick them up at the bus stop to bring them to our house. It was a long trip, but they never complained about coming to visit us. My parents had five other grandchildren at that time, but Johnny soon became one of their favorites. There was something about his smile that captured everyone's hearts. My mom and dad came to babysit for us many times and stayed over the weekends as well. Because of this, a special bond grew between Johnny and Grandma Fraterrigo. During the first few months with us, Johnny learned to speak a little and saying, "Gimma," made all four grandparents extremely happy.

CHAPTER

14

On one occasion while we were at my parents' home for dinner, Johnny tripped and somehow bit his tongue. The bite was bad enough to make it bleed. I don't know why, but he started pumping his tongue so that it bled even more. He swallowed the blood and then threw it up. I cleaned the mess, and we immediately left to go home. I wanted to get home ASAP in case it would happen again. I took one of Mom's big towels with us, and it was a good thing because just before we got to the George Washington Bridge, Johnny threw up again. We explained to the toll collector, and we asked if he could direct us to the nearest hospital. He arranged for a police escort, and we took Johnny to the emergency room in Teaneck Hospital.

The doctor there told us that there was nothing they could do for him and that the tongue needed to heal on its own. We got back in the car and drove home. Johnny slept most of the way, so he didn't pump his tongue again. After we got home, however, he started to pump his tongue again and up came the blood with other stuff with it as well. This time, it was worse than the first two. Thankfully we were in the kitchen where there was no carpeting. I had to get the biggest bath towel I had in order to clean it all up and then washed the floor. Even though it had gotten rather late, I called Dr. Roberts and got his answering service. I explained what happened, that it was urgent, and that I had to speak to the doctor ASAP. Not too long after, Dr. Roberts called us back. I repeated to him what had happened. He said that it probably looked worse than what it was, that there wasn't anything that could be done, and that he would come to the house first thing in the morning.

Johnny threw up one more time after I spoke with Dr. Roberts and again, I cleaned it up with another big bath towel and washed the floor.

Cleaning up all of this blood, and whatever else came up with it, was one of the hardest things I have ever done in my whole life. I was shaking; I was scared and could hardly believe what was happening. It started out as a bad dream, and it became a nightmare. My husband tried to help, but I thought it would be better if he just stood by Johnny to keep an eye on him. I'm sure that our son was just as frightened as we were and that he didn't know what was happening to him.

I couldn't put these big towels into the washing machine until I first got off all of the stuff from them. So I put them in the bathtub and cleaned them as best as I could. Then I had to go back and wash the floor to make sure that nothing had splashed onto the chairs or the walls. There was no way to know how much blood Johnny had lost, but it seemed to us that he couldn't have very much left. Our son's blood had been splattered all over the kitchen floor! Can you even begin to imagine what it was like for me to sop it all up? Unless you've been through it, you can't possibly imagine it, and I can't find the words to describe it. I can only tell you that the inner strength which I found coming from deep inside of me helped me to take care of the task at hand.

Johnny finally fell asleep at the table. My husband picked him up and laid him on the couch in the living room which was right next to the kitchen. We put a piece of plastic and a towel on the floor next to the couch just in case he needed it; but thank God, it didn't happen again. We both noticed, when he was lying on the couch, that Johnny was as pale as a ghost and looked like he was made out of wax. Luckily he slept through the rest of the night, and I slept on the couch next to him, both of us physically and emotionally exhausted.

The first thing in the morning, Dr. Roberts was at our door. When he came in and saw Johnny asleep on the couch, the look on his face showed that he couldn't believe what he saw. His words were, "Oh, my God! This is from a tongue bite?" He said that Johnny had to go to the hospital right away for a blood transfusion. He called the hospital to give them instructions, and my husband and I took Johnny to the emergency room at Valley Hospital in Ridgewood, New Jersey. They were waiting for us and took care of our son as soon as we got there.

Because they didn't know how much blood Johnny had lost, they had to do a transfusion and then check to see if he needed more. He also had to be fed intravenously in order to keep the tongue as still as possible so it would heal. They also kept him mildly sedated so that he wouldn't pull out the tubes for the transfusions or for the intravenous. I stayed as close to him as possible and from time to time, I'd put my hand on his head and stroked his hair just the way I did on his first night home. I said, "I think you like Mommy to do this."

From that time on, whenever he needed it, Johnny would take my hand and say, "Do this," and I knew what he meant. I don't recall how long he was in the hospital, but it was probably a day or two before he was able to come back home again.

CHAPTER

15

Time seemed to be going by quickly and before we knew it, summer had come. During these months, Johnny learned to enjoy sitting, splashing, and playing with rubber toys in a little inflatable pool which we bought and set up out in the backyard. We also bought him a bathing suit which looked like leopard skin and went up over one shoulder. What a handsome little boy he was!

Our little caveman.

Johnny also enjoyed our trips to the playground where there were swings and slides and a carousel similar to the one he rode on in Pat's backyard. Most of all, he loved going to Van Saun Park. We took him on the train ride which went all around the perimeter of the park, and then we went to look at the animals. There were sheep, goats, monkeys and other small animals. There were ducks swimming in a pond and chickens running around loose. But Johnny's favorites were the donkeys. For some reason, he seemed fascinated by donkeys. He would stare at them as though he was talking to them in his head. He'd have the biggest smile on his face like they were talking back to him. Who knows! Even when Johnny got older, whenever we went to a zoo no matter where we were, he couldn't wait to see the donkeys.

One summer afternoon, we decided to visit Grandma and Grandpa Artale in Brooklyn. We went by way of the West Side Drive in Manhattan which ran alongside of the Hudson River. There were a few motorboats and sailboats out on the water. I said to Johnny, who was sitting on my lap because there were no seatbelts back then, "Look at all the boats!" He looked out of the window, but there was a blank look on his face. I realized that he didn't know what a boat was. Soon after that, we bought him a couple of toy boats and showed him how to play with them in the water. The next time we drove on the West Side Drive, I again pointed out the boats to Johnny, and a big smile showed on his face. We had scored another win!

The rest of the summer went by visiting with friends and relatives, and they all fell in love with Johnny. His winning smile and big beautiful eyes captured everyone, and he enjoyed all of the attention that he got. There were also more train rides at the park, more visits to the zoo, and picnics, all of which Johnny really enjoyed. Before we knew it, autumn had replaced summer.

CHAPTER

16

One afternoon in October, Johnny was standing on the couch looking out of the big picture window which was right over the couch in our living room. When he turned around to get down, Johnny lost his balance and fell. His chin banged against the edge of the coffee table which was right next to the couch, and right below his lower lip, it began to bleed. I knew that Dr. Roberts had office hours that afternoon, so I quickly picked Johnny up and drove him there. Because of the urgency, the nurse had us go right in. The doctor saw that there was some bleeding inside of his mouth as well. He cleaned it out and cleared the clotted blood from the wound on his chin. It needed three stitches. Of course, Dr. Roberts first numbed the area in order to do anything and all in all, it went very well. I took Johnny home again. We'd have to wait to tell Daddy all about it when he got home from work.

Five days later, the three of us went back to have the stitches removed, and Johnny, being who he was, tugged at his chin and reopened the wound. This time, it didn't bleed; but the only way to hold it together again was with a big Band-Aid. Luckily Johnny didn't tug at it anymore, and it healed. However, it left a telltale scar on his chin which would always remind us of what happened that day.

CHAPTER 17

Six months had passed since we brought our son home that first day, and in six more months, the adoption would become legal. I thought that it was time for my husband and me to have a heart-to-heart talk. It was my observation that up until this point, even though he was helpful when help was needed, John was more of a spectator than a participant. Johnny was a whole lot different from the child whom we expected. Raising him would always be a challenge, and it would require much patience, acceptance, understanding of his disabilities, and a whole lot of love. We knew all of this when we first agreed not to give him up right at the beginning. However, now we were experiencing the reality of it, and Johnny needed to know, without a doubt, that he was wanted and loved. So we talked.

We spoke about things which were obvious. For instance, my husband would not be able to take Johnny to a ball game or go fishing with him, and our son would not be involved in Little League. Johnny wouldn't go to college or have a profession. He wouldn't get married nor have children. More than likely, we would have to accompany Johnny on a long journey of tests and examinations, finding and losing hope over and over again and would probably have much heartache along the way. The question was: can we truly accept this? So I asked John point-blank, "Can you be a father to this child?"

He answered, "I gave him my name, didn't I?" I wasn't quite ready for that answer and for a second or two, I froze. I couldn't believe what I'd heard. Then I said, "He already had a name. What he needs is a father who loves him and accepts him as he is." I couldn't talk anymore, so the conversation ended. We both had a lot to think about now.

Apparently our talk was a turning point because my husband opened his heart and his mind, turned things around, and became the father that Johnny needed. He paid more attention to him, playing with him, reading to him, taking him for walks, and showing him lots of affection.

CHAPTER

18

It was fall. We had a large twin oak tree in our backyard which shed its leaves and enabled us to rake them up into big piles, jump into them, throw them up into the air, and watch them fall down around us. Like teaching Johnny how to play with toys, I had to go first. When he watched me play in the leaves, he was convinced that it might be a fun thing to do, and he finally tried it. He got the idea, and we played in the leaves together until we got tired. Remember, every time we jumped on the pile of leaves, we had to rake them back together.

When Halloween came, there were lots of children coming to our door for trick or treat. I could tell by the expression on his face that Johnny didn't understand what these children were doing, so I tried to explain it to him. I don't think he liked the idea of my giving away his candy but after the first few, I got him to help me give out the treats. When he got older, we dressed him up in a costume and took him around to a few neighbors. He got to like Halloween and filling up his bag with candy.

Before we knew it, the holidays were upon us. The first Thanksgiving with Johnny was a real celebration for us. We invited both our families for dinner. My two brothers came, each with their wife and three children, also my mother-in-law and father-in-law, and my mom and dad who came a couple of days earlier so that Mom could give me a hand with all of the preparations.

Italian holiday meals are an all-day extravaganza. Not so much these days but back then, we started with antipasto then came the soup. You had to have a pasta dish, followed by the main course which, for this holiday, was turkey with all of the trimmings. The meal wouldn't be complete without fruit, nuts, pastries, and coffee.

With so much food, it's no wonder it took all day. We ate in phases. The first one ended after the pasta. The best part of the day was having the whole family together and the fun we had. Johnny especially enjoyed watching everybody having a good time. He got to know his cousins who didn't know how to act toward him at first. Johnny was different. He didn't speak and kind of shied away from them, clinging on to me. Little by little, with patience and encouragement, he accepted them into his world and they accepted him into theirs.

Christmas was a little different. On Christmas Eve, we went to Brooklyn to be with Mom and Dad Artale's family for dinner. We were seventeen people all together. The traditional Italian custom of a meal with seven fishes is what was served for dinner. Of course, we also had antipasto and a pasta dish. Once again, Johnny had to work his way into a family gathering, and we all had a good time. Most of all, Johnny enjoyed tearing the paper off of his presents.

On Christmas day, we opened our presents the first thing in the morning; and one by one, Johnny enjoyed tearing the paper off of them. Eventually he started to play with his toys. After breakfast, we got dressed and went to Mass. We then ventured way out to Long Island to spend Christmas Day with my family, this time, at my brother's house. Another big meal and more presents. It was a long trip after a long day, and Johnny slept most of the way coming home. New Year's Eve and Day were quiet for us. The hectic holiday season came to an end, and we wondered what the New Year would have in store for us.

CHAPTER

19

In 1962, two different but equally important events took place. First of all, our trial period came to an end. It was time for Johnny's adoption to become legal. Secondly Johnny started nursery school.

The first few months went by quickly. Johnny continued to learn some new words and new things and adapted well to his new life. My husband and I also had to adapt to our new life. Teaching Johnny required lots of our time and patience, and there were times when it wasn't easy. There are no courses in school which teaches prospective parents how to raise children. It's a learn-as-you-go process. Teaching children with learning disabilities brings additional challenges to the process. However, with a great deal of love, we were able to move forward together.

Finally in July, we received a letter from our lawyer letting us know that our adoption hearing was scheduled for August 13 at 9:30 a.m. at the Bergen County Courthouse in Hackensack, New Jersey. All went well, and we were now legally the Artale family: my husband, myself, and our son, John. In September, we received both a copy of Johnny's birth certificate, a copy of the Judgment of Adoption, and his passport which included the first picture we saw of Johnny when we had our meeting with Ms. Neilson at Catholic Charities. We were informed that two years from the date of judgment, we could apply to have Johnny become a citizen of the USA. We were to contact the naturalization clerk at the county courthouse in June 1964 in order to get the necessary forms and directions as to what we had to do. Shortly after the legal proceedings were completed, we contacted Catholic Charities and informed them that we were anxious to adopt another child. This time, we asked for a girl under the age of one year.

Once again, we had to fill out forms for Catholic Charities and meet all of their requirements. They also requested a letter from Johnny's doctor. The letter was necessary because there was no medical record stating that Johnny had neurological disorders. Dr. Roberts responded to Catholic Charities with a letter which included the fact that Johnny's disorder was evident to him from the first time he saw him, and that it was something which should have been noted by whoever examined him even before he was put up for adoption so that the adoptive parents would be advised of his neurological condition. He also stated that Johnny was doing as well as could be expected under the circumstances and that he was making good progress under our excellent care of him. We appreciated that statement very much, and I'm sure that Ms. Nielson made note of it.

In anticipation of our second adoption, we decided to expand our attic. We had the roof opened up at the back of the house and added a dormer large enough for two bedrooms and a bath. It wasn't completed until five years later when we finally needed it.

The second event that year, 1962, Johnny was enrolled in the Alice in Wonderland Nursery School. When I started to write about this, I asked myself, "Why did I do it?" I thought about it and finally remembered what led up to it. I spent most of my day with Johnny. He liked music, so I tried teaching him little songs which he enjoyed. He would wait until I came to the end of the song, and then he would add his two notes and clap his hands. I showed him how to build with blocks, and he laughed when they came tumbling down. We played little games like Ring Round the Rosie and Itsy-Bitsy Spider. I read to him, and "did this" when he got tired. I couldn't recall everything about that time fifty years ago, but I did remember the following incident.

One hot summer day, Johnny was having one of his bad days when nothing seemed to please him. I was telling my neighbor Barbara, and she said that she would make some lemonade, bring it over, and we would sit outside under the tree and relax. Sounded good to me; so she came over with the lemonade. Johnny, however, didn't stop bugging me, so I poured out the remainder of my drink on top of his head. He was stunned by this, and I couldn't believe that I did it. I hugged him and said that I was sorry, but the deed had been done. After that, he behaved the rest of the afternoon. It was then that Barbara suggested that I enroll Johnny in nursery school so that I'd have a couple of hours to myself. I talked it over with my husband, and we decided to give it a try. It was a major adjustment for both Johnny and me. I spoke with the teacher about Johnny and his problems, and she allowed me to stay with him the first day. When I left him the next day, I told him that I would be back to pick him up to bring him home. I felt confident that he'd be all right without me. The teacher was very patient with him and tried to encourage him to join in the activities with the other children, but she said that he didn't seem at all interested. Each day when I picked him up, the teacher gave me a report on whether Johnny was either cooperative or disruptive. Eventually he made an adjustment and continued there until March of 1964. All things considered, he seemed happy, and I got the break that I needed.

During that time, the teacher noted that Johnny held things quite close to his eyes and suggested that we have his eyes examined. We made an appointment with Dr. Wilder, an ophthalmologist, and took him in for an examination. Obviously Johnny couldn't play the "E game," so the doctor would show him an object and then put it down somewhere close by in the room, or he'd drop it on the floor and have Johnny retrieve it. The doctor was also able to look into Johnny's eyes as best as Johnny would allow him to, and he was able to come up with a diagnosis. He determined that Johnny had paralysis of the ciliary muscle of the eye and that because of this, the curvature of the lens could no longer be adjusted to focus on nearby objects. He also said that he had a primary optic atrophy. Eyeglasses were not an option. The last comment that Dr. Wilder made before we left was that he thought it might be possible, because of his neurological impairment, that as Johnny learned more, he would see more. I remembered back to the time when Johnny could see the boats in the river only after he learned what a boat was. What the doctor said turned out to be true.

CHAPTER

20

It was in the summer of 1963 when we visited a school friend of mine with whom I still kept in touch. Her name is Rose Marie. She married a man who was a pediatrician and is now retired. They had five children, four boys and a girl, who have grown up to be fine young men and woman. We enjoyed our visit very much. Johnny didn't mingle with the other children but all in all, we had an enjoyable visit.

During the course of the day, Gene, Rose Marie's husband, had been observing Johnny and suggested that we take him to see a doctor friend of his, Dr. Lawrence Shaw. At the time, Dr. Shaw was the Associate Director of the Department of Pediatrics and Pediatric Rehabilitation at the Albert Einstein College of Medicine in the Bronx, New York. He was top in the profession and highly respected. Gene said that he would get in touch with Dr. Shaw and advise him that we would be calling for an appointment. We appreciated the referral, and soon after our visit, we called Dr. Shaw and set up an appointment for December 2. He asked that Dr. Roberts send him a letter with Johnny's medical background which he did.

Upon our visit with Dr. Shaw, we found him to be everything we expected him to be. He had a pleasant personality, was informative and sympathetic to our situation. His neurological examination had to be somewhat limited because of Johnny's resistance to it. Nevertheless, with his observations and limited examination of Johnny, Dr. Shaw was able to come up with a diagnosis. He said that we were dealing with an autistic youngster. However, he also noted there were times during the visit when Johnny would stop what he was doing and stare in a trance-like state as though he was looking through you. Because of this, Dr. Shaw thought it would be worthwhile to get an EEG on Johnny in order to rule out some type of petit mal attack. He knew of a youngster who had petit mal attacks with no evidence of seizure disorder but who acted for many years as an autistic child. We had the EEG done, and Dr. Shaw telephoned us when he got the results. He explained that the test showed diffused abnormalities, meaning that the damage was not only in one area, but spread out to different parts of the brain. Only 10% of the brain was neurologically damaged, but because it was diffused, Johnny's brain had limited intake and output capabilities. This meant that he could learn things, but wouldn't always be able to tell you what he knew. Dr. Shaw said that this type of brain damage usually occurred from a traumatic injury to the head, or other interference with the development of the brain when it is being formed. In Johnny's case, this is most likely when it occurred.

Dr. Shaw also thought that an appropriate type of placement in a class for neurologically-impaired children might work for Johnny if it was possible to get him enrolled in one. In the event that it didn't work out for him, then Johnny might require residential placement. We would have to wait and see. There was no question in Dr. Shaw's mind, however, considering Johnny's background, that his whole condition could be due to one of maternal deprivation. He did say that the prognosis was poor, but he did not leave us without hope.

CHAPTER
21

In March '64, Johnny would no longer be attending the Alice in Wonderland Nursery School, so I contacted the assistant superintendent of education of the Fair Lawn School District. I wrote that my husband and I hoped that in September, we would be enrolling our son in the special classes of the school's education system. However, in the meantime, since our son was entitled to schooling, we requested that for the balance of the school year, the board of education would approve his attendance at a nursery school which was conducted by the Bergen-Passaic Unit of the New Jersey Association for Retarded Children. The nearest one was located at the Church of the Good Shepherd in Midland Park. Therefore, the board would also have to provide transportation for Johnny to and from the school.

Two weeks later, I received a response to my letter stating that Johnny's medical records would be needed in order for a complete evaluation to be made and that the records should be released to Mrs. Marion Channing, the school psychologist. At the same time, they would be exploring the possibility of placing Johnny in a class for neurologically-impaired children in September. We were assured that serious consideration was being given to ways in which our son might best be served in the Fair Lawn school system.

Two weeks later, Mrs. Channel received the information from Dr. Roberts. He stated that an EEG taken in December 1963 showed diffused abnormalities. His diagnosis was that "Johnny was a neurologically-impaired child with psychiatric problems most likely based on early maternal deprivation when he was in an orphanage." Dr. Roberts also stated that "although Johnny's prognosis was poor, he had improved considerably over the past three years since he first saw him due to admirable care given to him by his parents."

After all was said and done, Johnny started nursery school at the Church of the Good Shepherd in April with transportation being provided by the Fair Lawn School District. At the end of the school year, I received the following report of Johnny's progress over the time he spent there. I'm quoting the report just as it was written to me.

> When John first came to school, he stood alone on the playground and wouldn't go inside the classroom. I knew that he liked water so I brought out a basin of water, showed it to John, and told him to come inside. He followed the water that I carried into the classroom and started playing with it. He always put his face down to the level of the water in order to see it. I feel that he cannot see well. Whenever John wet himself with the water, he completely undressed himself. When we tried to redress him in dry clothes, he screamed and screeched. He resisted all attempts to dress him.
>
> I assigned my 15-year-old daughter, Susan, to watch him every morning to see that he would not hurt himself or anyone else. She was with him all the time.
>
> Every day when he came to school, he sought out Susan and gave her a basin to be filled with water. Sometimes she gave him 3 or 4 basins, plastic bottles, floating toys and soap suds. He poured and emptied the water from container to container. Sometimes he purposely poured the water on the floor from all the basins. When this happened, we removed all the basins, and John screamed and screamed and could not be stopped. After several days of this I said, "Johnny stop screaming or I'll put soap in your mouth." I put soap in his mouth and he didn't like the taste so he started to cry, "no scream—no soap."

He understood what I had done. On other days when he found himself screaming, he repeated, "no scream—no soap." On occasion I had to remind him that if he screamed, I would put soap in his mouth. Once he learned not to scream, we could understand better what he wanted, and he spoke more.

Sometimes John would be on the playground, just looking. One day Susan picked him up bodily and put him on a bicycle. She held his hands on the handle grips and put his feet on the pedals. After a while, he pedaled himself. That same day, he took a doll and put her on the bike and held her hands on the handle grips. A few days later he got on the bike with the doll, put his hands and the doll's hands on the handles, and tried to ride this way!

He liked a pegboard that could be filled with plastic flowers. The flowers had sharp prongs that fitted into the pegboard. When John came to school he looked for this toy. He looked on all the shelves until he found it. He felt the prongs with his fingertips before he fitted them into the pegboard.

One morning, Susan lifted John up on a high rung of the jungle gym and she got up with him to watch him. He climbed down carefully, and then he followed Susan all over the jungle gym and smiled and seemed very happy.

At the beginning, John never seemed to notice the children and never sat with a group. He just walked around and did not notice anyone. As time went on, he sat on a chair and sang certain songs with the children. When they sang, "Pop Goes the Weasel", John got very excited anticipating the moment when the children clapped and shouted "pop." He ran to the front of the group in anticipation and then smiled after the pop.

School lasted only six weeks. By the sixth week, Susan did not have to watch him. John had stopped screaming. If he wanted something, he would search for Susan and say, "doggie" (a petal game), or "bubbles." If he wanted the record player, he would look for it and find records and play with the records. One little boy used to take the records from John. John would push him away from the record player. The other children who came over just to listen to the records were never bothered by John.

John seemed very relaxed and happy during the last days of school. I felt this would be a time for him to learn specific skills, but I do not have the training, and the school year was at its end."

I'm so glad that Johnny had the opportunity to attend the Church of the Good Shepherd Nursery School. He did so well there that I only wish he had gone there right from the beginning of the school year instead of at the end.

CHAPTER
22

Some things come to you when you least expect it. We had been waiting for months to hear from Catholic Charities regarding our second application for adoption. Then one day in March 1964, I received a phone call from Ms. Nielson. I was surprised to hear from her and wondered what additional information she needed regarding our application. I was even more surprised when she told me that she had a beautiful, healthy baby girl, only eight weeks old, which she felt would be a perfect match for us. She also said that if we were interested, we could come in at any time, fill out the necessary papers, and take her home. You could have knocked me over with a feather. I was speechless. My mind started racing. We weren't prepared. I told her that the answer was yes and that I'd call her back the next day after I spoke to my husband, and we'd let her know when we could come in.

The first thing I did was phone John at work to give him the good news. When he answered the phone, I said, "Guess what? You're going to be the father of a beautiful baby girl!" I could hear the excitement in his voice when he announced the news to everyone in the office. Next I phoned our parents and a few other people including our neighbor Alice to ask if her daughter Rita could come over to babysit after supper so that John and I could go out shopping for baby things. She was very happy to say yes! Rita was the oldest of seven daughters. She loved babysitting for Johnny, and he liked it when she came over to stay with him.

When Johnny came home from school, I told him that he was going to have a baby sister and that he would be her big brother. I tried to explain to him even though I knew he wouldn't quite understand, what it would be like to have a little baby in our family, and I hoped that when the time came, he would be all right with it.

That night after supper, Rita came over to babysit, and John and I went out shopping. We bought a basinet, a changing table, baby clothes, blankets, and everything else that was necessary in order to bring our daughter home. The next day, I phoned Ms. Nielson to tell her that we definitely wanted to make an appointment to see her as soon as possible and to make all of the necessary arrangements. The day came, and filled with joy, we brought Regina Maria home.

Regina was a delight. Having a little baby to love and care for was everything I had always hoped for and waited so long for. It was a challenge, however, trying to juggle my time between Johnny and Regina. Both needed my full attention, sometimes at the same time. Johnny didn't pay much attention to Regina. He was curious at first especially whenever she cried. I explained to him that when she cried, she was either hungry or she needed a diaper change or something was upsetting her and that we had to find out what it was and fix it to make her happy again. After a while, Johnny's curiosity was satisfied and even though he didn't seem to care much about her, he always seemed to be watching her out of the corner of his eye.

Regina was a happy baby. She had a smile for everyone. She was smart and a fast learner. Regina walked and spoke a few words before she was a year old. Our parents were crazy about her as were all of our relatives and friends. We knew, of course, that our first year together was a trial period, and we also knew that unless a disaster occurred, Regina would legally become a part of our family.

CHAPTER
23

In the same month that we brought Regina home, we received a letter from the Fair Lawn School's assistant superintendent of education, informing us that based on all of the information regarding our son, they did not have the proper facilities in the school system that would best serve him. It was recommended that we make application for admission to the Forum School in Paramus which was a school for children with similar disabilities and would be a more suitable situation. Dr. Roberts was contacted, and he agreed with the recommendation. He forwarded Johnny's medical records to the Fair Lawn school psychologist along with a letter which said:

> The parents have cared for this youngster most admirably. He has improved considerably over the past three years. His prognosis is poor, and extreme difficulty still exists. My diagnosis is a neurologically impaired child, with psychiatric problems, based on maternal deprivation when he was in an orphanage for the first three years of his life.

The spring and summer of 1964 was a period of adjustment for all of us. With the help of my parents, who visited on weekends whenever they could, and Rita, our babysitter, everything went very well. When September came, Johnny went to the Forum School for a few hours a day, and I was able to enjoy Regina without splitting myself in two.

In October, we contacted the Immigration and Naturalization Service, US Department of Justice on Johnny's behalf in order to start the proceedings for him to become a citizen of the USA. There were many papers to fill out which included documenting the last five years of our residence and employment. We had to include proof of our marriage, evidence that we were able to support and care for him, and a certified copy of the adoption agreement. They also required a recent photograph of Johnny, faced front and without a hat.

Only one of us could be designated as the petitioner. I was the one most available so as the petitioner, my fingerprints had to be submitted for a background check.

After all was said and done, Johnny became a citizen in December 1964. In February 1965, the governor of the state of New Jersey, Richard Hughes, sent a letter to Master John Artale, congratulating him on becoming a citizen of the USA.

CHAPTER
24

It so happened that on October 15 that same year, there was an article in the newspaper which caught my attention. The headline read, "Hundreds of Brain-Injured Youngsters Are Conquering Handicaps Through This Unique Treatment at the Institutes for the Achievement of Human Potential in Philadelphia, PA." The article was extensive with photos of half a dozen children of various ages undergoing therapy treatment, and they were getting marvelous results.

The institute had its beginnings in 1955 with Glenn Doman as the director. To my knowledge as of this writing, he is still at the institute. He and a group of doctors including neurosurgeons, psychologists, educators, physical and speech therapists, a specialist in physical medicine, and a nurse made up the team which worked together to develop the program. It took more than two decades of research into the causes and treatment of brain damage after which they concluded that brain injury did not originate in any part of the body other than in the brain itself and that it is the brain which must be treated. A professor of neurosurgery at Temple University had noted that most brain injuries did not involve the destruction of all of the cells in the injured area. He suggested that it might be possible to activate the millions of surviving cells to take over the function of the dead ones. The team concluded that the program they devised, which if followed, would allow this transfer to take place.

The article mentioned that the problems could possibly be with the incoming or outgoing pathways to the brain. It also stated that the brain can suffer because of an injury or experience which happened to the mother as the baby was developing or if oxygen is cut off or decreased for any reason. The incident which caused the injury is over, but the outcome, however, may not become apparent until later on in life. What is left is a good brain that has gotten hurt and needs help. The article mentioned that 70 percent of children could be helped and that 30 percent would not qualify.

Was this the answer to our prayers? Which group would Johnny fit into? I wondered if he would even be eligible for evaluation at the institute.

I was afraid of another discouragement, but every time I read another one of their articles, I couldn't help but wonder whether or not there would really be help available from the source which I was afraid to approach. Finally, even though at the time there was a four-year waiting period, in February 1967, I wrote a three-page letter to Mr. Doman, the director of the institutes, telling him about our son, John. I will come back to this again later on in my writing. Meanwhile you can learn more about the IAHP on their website. There's a lot more information available now than there was back in 1964.

CHAPTER

25

Having a baby in the house made things somewhat more challenging. The year 1964 was a period of adjustments. Like all other families, we had our ups and downs; but all in all, things were going quite well.

In 1965, two happy occasions took place. The first was on May 4, when Regina legally became part of our family. The other, that Johnny was approved for admission to the class for trainable children at the Roosevelt School in Fair Lawn, and he started there in September. His teacher, Mrs. Wilson, really loved her work and the children she taught. It seemed that Johnny was adjusting well and that he was getting along very well with her. However, 1966 presented a very different story which started a chain of events that would ultimately take us in a totally different direction.

CHAPTER 26

The year began when I received a letter from Mrs. Wilson. In essence, what the letter said was that it seemed as though my temper and emotions were affecting Johnny. She suggested that I pray for patience, endurance, and self-control when dealing with him at home. She wrote that Johnny was so upset when he got to school that he grabbed toys and other materials away from the other children and threw them about the room. He screamed a lot and seemed ready to tear everything and everybody apart.

Johnny only went to school part of the time, and Mrs. Wilson indicated that she had to plan her schedule so that certain activities would be over before he arrived. She also wrote, and I quote:

> Basically, Johnny seems to be such a sweet child that to me it would seem a shame on your part not to be able to cultivate enough self-control, understanding, and patience with him, to allow his better qualities to develop fully. Whenever you are tempted to spank or scream at him, could you possibly try to put yourself in his place and down to his size and age, consider well all that he says and does, and decide on the kind of reaction you would like to expect from "Mommy".

When I was writing this book, I was trying to remember why I would've gotten such a letter from Mrs. Wilson. I know that I wouldn't spank or scream at Johnny before sending him to school. However, I did remember that I was very stressed out back then. I was dealing with Johnny day to day, never knowing what to expect next, and also dealing with a very active two-year-old daughter who also needed lots of my attention. On top of that, my husband John and I were going through a rough time in our relationship.

Johnny was my barometer. If I was in a good mood, so was he. If I was in a bad mood, so was he. If I was stressed out, he would feel it as well. Johnny wasn't able to verbally express his thoughts or feelings. He did it by his actions. That's probably what was happening at school.

Mrs. Wilson scheduled a parent-teacher conference a few days after I received her letter. I was able to meet with her, and we had a very long discussion about Johnny. We talked about many things, and we both left the meeting agreeing to work together to help Johnny along. We kept in contact and kept updated on his progress and any problems that came up. In March, I received another note from Mrs. Wilson. This time it read, "Johnny seems happy, relaxed and cooperative in school."

Johnny had a book which had 365 days of the year in it with pictures and little stories describing each of the pictures. I used to give him the book every day when he came home from school. He sat at the kitchen table and enjoyed looking through it. One day, I was standing at the kitchen sink. It was the month of February. I don't remember what I was doing, but I heard Johnny say, "Abraham Lincoln." I thought I was hearing things. I went over to the table and saw that Johnny was looking at a picture of Abraham Lincoln. I asked him who that was, and he repeated the name. I was totally surprised. I decided to turn the page to find George Washington and pointed to him. I asked Johnny who that was and he said, "George Washington." I could hardly believe my eyes, but there he was, George Washington. I gave Johnny a big hug and told him that I was so proud of him and how happy he made me feel. I couldn't wait for my husband to get home from work so that he could share in the good news. However, Johnny never repeated it again. It was as though it had never happened.

CHAPTER
27

In April '66, Johnny, for no known reason, decided to go on a hunger strike. He absolutely refused to eat anything. We took him to Dr. Roberts who said that he could find nothing physically wrong with him and that when he got hungry enough, he would start eating again. In the meantime, we were to give him Instant Breakfast as much as he would take each day. Well, Johnny's hunger strike lasted for three months. He survived on Instant Breakfast and water. He lost so much weight that his body looked as bad as when we first brought him home. He was skin and bones and every time I bathed him, tears ran down my face. He was so weak that he could hardly speak or move on his own. Finally Dr. Roberts had us bring him to Presbyterian Hospital in New York City where he was admitted with a diagnosis of anorexia of three months' duration.

While at the hospital, which lasted from June 30 to July 15, Johnny was seen by four different doctors and underwent all kinds of X-rays, lab tests, EKGs, and EEGs. The results showed a slight abnormal EKG. Also psychiatric and neurologic consultation showed evidence of diffused brain damage with retardation and autism. During hospitalization, Johnny continued to eat only jelly, ice cream, and coke. The doctors suggested institutional care and discharged him. At some point in August, as mysteriously as it started, Johnny began eating again. It took about a year or so to get him back to his normal weight.

CHAPTER

28

The doctor's words, "institutional care," were weighing me down. My husband, John, and I talked about it many times, and we kept coming up with the same decision. Unless things got out of hand and we could no longer care for Johnny at home, we wouldn't even consider placing him elsewhere. We would do everything we could to not let that happen.

In September, we were contacted by Ms. Updike from the New Jersey Bureau of Mental Retardation, again stressing the importance of placing Johnny in an outside-the-home facility as soon as possible. I told her that we were not ready to do that and after our conversation, she gave me the name of the county supervisor of child study, Mr. John Mangan, and where to reach him. On October 27, I wrote a letter to him informing him of Johnny's current situation in school and that we were hoping a new program could be set up for him which would include adding one more hour to his day, possibly as a one-on-one with another teacher. To date, he was attending school for three hours a day, and he had not received any physical education, music, art, or speech therapy, and we thought that this could be incorporated into his program.

In November, we received a letter from the acting superintendent of schools in Fair Lawn, stating that re-evaluation of John's school program showed agreement by the classroom teacher, supplementary teacher, and psychologist, that no change should be made at the time. So everything remained the same.

CHAPTER

29

My next step was to write to the State Commissioner of Education in Trenton, New Jersey. I wrote the letter to him on November 10, and once again explained our son's current situation regarding the education program set up for him in the Fair Lawn school system. My husband and I were asking whether something more could be provided for him according to the Beadleston Act of 1954 (changed in 1997 to be known as the Individual with Disabilities Education Act), which required "a greater level of services be provided to special education pupils than federal regulations requirements." I included a copy of my letter to Mr. Mangan.

On December 27, I received a letter from the Bergen County Department of Education, stating that an appointment would be set up with the Assistant Superintendent in Fair Lawn to discuss the program designed for our son. It was signed by "John Mangan, State Child Study Supervisor." The meeting was held in February '67 and as a result, Fair Lawn would look into the possibility of Johnny entering, the At-The-Cliffs school in Westwood, New Jersey, which was a school for children with special needs. Their primary goal was "to habilitate each youngster to appreciate his own worth and function adequately within his own scope. The program is designed to develop the skills, habits, and attitudes that build confidence, foster independence, and encourage responsibility." Johnny would attend the school for two hours per day for the '67–'68 school year.

CHAPTER
30

Several other things took place in the interim. In June 1966, John received his first Holy Communion. One of the nuns in our parish, Sister Colum, used to talk to John when we took him to church on Sundays. She asked us for permission to work with him so that he would be able to receive his first communion. Of course, we were delighted.

For those who don't know, in order to receive communion in the Roman Catholic Church, you must believe, or in John's case at least recognize, the true presence of Jesus in the host you are receiving. My husband and I wondered how she would be able to accomplish it. She said, "Don't worry. You'll see!" After working with John, the time came when she said that he was ready. She invited us to come to his lesson so that we could see the results. Sister Colum took a host and asked John, "What is this?"

He answered, "Bread."

Then she explained to John what the priest was going to do next, and the prayers he would say, after which Sister asked John again, "What is this?"

And with a smile, he answered, "Jesus!"

Yes, he was ready to receive his first Holy Communion. However, we wondered whether or not he would be able to sit through a whole Mass without being disruptive. Well, one of our priests, Father Jordan Charbonneau, offered to have us bring John to church at a time other than Mass and that he would be happy to say a few prayers and have John receive Communion one-on-one. Father said, "If I have to call on every saint in heaven for help, I will do it because today, John will receive his first Holy Communion."

Problem solved. Thanks to Sister Colum and Father Jordan, all went well, and everyone was happy and proud of John.

In July of 1967, John received a certificate for his participation in the YMCA Swim Program. He didn't learn how to swim, but he was not afraid to get in and out of the pool by himself, and he moved his arms and legs with some assistance. Many people take these things for granted, but for John, this was an accomplishment, and it made him and us proud.

Also in July, John was accepted to attend Camp Beacon, a summer-camp program which was run by the New Jersey Association for Brain-Injured Children in Paramus, New Jersey, for the specific development of the child through recreation. It was supervised by a professional staff. It provided an experience in an environment which did not compete with the school program but was in contrast to the time spent in programs that were frustrating to the child because of the expectations put upon that child in a classroom setting.

It was a rustic setting with opportunities for cookouts, hiking, games, swimming, and other camp events. The senior counselors were teachers who were active in special education with junior counselors to assist them. The ratio of counselor to camper was three-to-one which made room for one-on-one when necessary. There was a qualified swimming instructor and a full-time nurse to administer required medication and to maintain a first-aid station. Transportation was provided at centrally-located pick-up points to and from the camp. At the end of the season, parents were to be provided with the counselor's observations and comments regarding the child's achievements, behavior, reactions, and adjustments to the program, the campers, and the camp life at Beacon. It seemed like an ideal place for Johnny.

These are brief comments made by the counselor who worked with him.

> Johnny appears to prefer a one-on-one relationship with a female. He was adamant about having his own seat on the bus. He had relatively few fears, however, he had a fear of heights, which

subsided considerably during the time he worked with a counselor. Johnny played well beside other children, but made no apparent attempt to play with them. He enjoyed and did well on much of the playground equipment. One of the counselors helped Johnny to eat his lunch and use the bathroom by offering swimming as a reward. He resisted formal instruction in swimming, but enjoyed being in the water. Johnny did not care to sing, but became very interested in hand motions which accompanied some of the songs.

All in all, my husband and I were pleased with the report we got and agreed that Johnny did well at Camp Beacon. There was one incident, however, which I remember most vividly. It was on a day when I went to visit the camp. I don't remember why I was there. It may have been a day for parents to visit. Whatever it was, I was watching Johnny, enjoying playing in the water, when I noticed a change coming over him. I knew that he was about to have a seizure. I immediately called out to the counselor who quickly got him out of the water. She laid him in my arms, and I carried him, who was dead weight, as fast as I could and ran with him to the first-aid station. He rested there for a while, and then I dressed him and took him home with me. I was a little nervous about sending him to camp the next day, but I felt confident that he was in good hands and that his guardian angel would be watching over him. Thank God there were no more incidents for the rest of the camp season.

CHAPTER
31

Earlier in my writing, I referred to a letter which I wrote in February 1967 to Mr. Glenn Domen, director of the Institute for the Achievement of Human Potential. When I was reading that letter again, I was surprised at some of the things I had written to Mr. Domen. I hadn't remembered all of the progress Johnny had made in the years since we adopted him.

When we first took him home, he was not able to speak, was not toilet-trained, could just about walk straight, couldn't dress or feed himself, would never look straight ahead at anything or anyone, and he didn't know how to play with toys. He understood every word spoken to him in Italian, so we spoke Italian to him for a few days and then switched to English. He quickly responded not only to a new language but to a new environment and most of all, to a new name from Mario to Johnny. Within the first year with us, he was completely toilet-trained, was trying and learning how to speak; he could walk without tripping or bumping into things. He could feed himself with a spoon, and he began helping to dress himself. He learned how to play with a ball, a truck, and a few other toys as well.

By the time I wrote the letter, because of his schooling and working with my husband and me at home, Johnny could speak in very small sentences; he could jump, attempt to skip and hop, had good balance, could ride a tricycle, and could dress mostly by himself. Johnny's eye-hand coordination was improving. He could put together wooden inlaid puzzles of about twenty-five pieces rather quickly. He could draw straight lines, circles, rectangles, triangles, and was beginning to draw objects such as a dog, truck, boy, and a food tray. Johnny seemed to enjoy looking through books and magazines, would identify objects and compare them to things around the house.

I didn't know how long we would have to wait for a response to my letter because of the four-year waiting period mentioned in the article I had read about the institute. We weren't even sure that we would get a response at all. However, three months later, on May 22, we got a letter from a Mrs. Davis, the clinical coordinator at the institute, acknowledging receipt of our request for an appointment. The letter stated that they were deluged with requests and were limited to scheduling approximately 350 children a year, and that the first possible available time when they could see our son would be on March 24, 1969. They acknowledged that it was an unreasonable waiting period but urged us to accept the appointment and confirm it with them. They would notify us if an earlier appointment would become available.

We were very excited to have received a response in a rather short period of time and confirmed the date right away. Now we had to play the waiting game; but as you will see, it wouldn't be at all boring.

CHAPTER
32

In September of that year, we received a letter from the Fair Lawn Board of Education, informing us that John was approved to attend the At-The-Cliffs School for the 1967–68 school year. He would be attending from 9:00–11:00 a.m., and transportation would be provided for him. The staff at the school worked with children who had various disabilities, and they worked in small groups of four to five, and if necessary, on a one-on-one basis. A highly-trained staff of teachers and therapists were employed by the school, and my husband and I were very happy that our son would be attending there.

John started out in a small group. Everything was new to him, and he didn't want to be there. He reacted by screaming, crying, hitting, biting, and throwing things around. They tried working with him but after the first month, it was decided that he would do better with a one-on-one teacher. John was assigned to work with Anthony Capisano and as it turned out, they couldn't have chosen a better teacher for him.

Mr. Capisano sent John home, almost every day, with a note telling me about the things that John did or didn't do; whether or not he was interactive with him or any of the other children. Occasionally Mr. Capisano would request a response from me as to how John was doing at home. We were able to establish a great relationship via these notes.

John was adjusting so well that after one month, his hours at school were increased to a full day. He was involved with many activities, one-on-one and in small groups. John showed resistance at first in speech class, but within two months, he was naming pictures and using one-to-several words in sentences. In music class, he began singing small phrases of songs. He especially enjoyed the "Indian Song," which included some hand motions. One of his favorite things was playing on the trampoline. He was very possessive of it at first, but then he let the other children play on it also. He showed interest in looking at books. He was following instructions and completing simple tasks by himself. John could put different shapes into their right place and could put big wooden puzzles together quite well. He knew different colors, and he enjoyed painting and stringing beads.

At the end of October, Mr. Capisano wrote in a summary report:

> John has become more open. He talks more, responds better, there is a decrease in negative behavior. A positive approach—that of approval—has been applied, and much affection has helped John. He has made a beautiful adjustment in all areas.

Things continued to improve during the months of November and December. He was smiling more, not as withdrawn, and making better eye contact. However, in January, things began to change.

CHAPTER 33

At first, John seemed very happy to be back in school after the holiday break; but by the end of the month, he was not responding as well as before. He seemed disturbed and withdrawn. Mr. Capisano wanted to know if John was on a new medication, but there had been no changes at that time. There were days when John was reachable and days when he was very disruptive in class and difficult to discipline. This, of course, reflected on his ability to achieve his goals in class and this continued into February. A brief mention here that something new was now added to John's day—crawling. He was to do some crawling at school and continue it at home as well. He didn't like it and wasn't very cooperative. After a while, it was discontinued.

Even though John's behavior was like a roller coaster at that time, he was making progress in some areas. He was learning how to draw squares and color them in; he was learning how to make the letters of his name; he enjoyed picking up books and looking at the pictures and had an interest in drawing a man and naming the parts of the body. John was singing songs like "Mary Had a Little Lamb" which he hadn't done in a long time. He was talking more, telling his age, what he was looking at, and following instructions better. He was enjoying putting wooden puzzles together and doing them well. Mr. Capisano sent home a note which read, "John has moments when he's very cooperative. Firmness done in a calm, quiet voice has helped him. He has much latent knowledge which could be developed further, but he has such a short attention span that it's difficult to get him to produce."

Regina and her big brother.

At home, he was playing more with Regina. He also brought a book to me and asked me to "read the book" with him. However, John's behavior was getting harder for us to handle. Rather than repressing his anger, he was expressing it. This, in and of itself, was a good thing for him but difficult for us. He'd be going along just great and from out of nowhere, he seemed to get angry and would act up a storm. When it was over, it was as though it had never happened. You knew that he was angry but not why.

Once we were at the table, eating dinner, and like a flash, John pushed back his chair, ran to the refrigerator, and swung open the door with such force that it was tipping forward. Some of the food slipped off from the front of the shelves. If my husband hadn't jumped up after him to hold it back, the fridge could've fallen on him and caused serious injury. On another occasion, I heard Regina, who was now four years old, let out a loud cry. I ran to see what had happened. She had fallen down the stairs. She said that John had pushed her. He was standing at the top of the stairs chuckling. First I made sure that Regina was all right and then quickly ran up the stairs. I took John by the hand to his room and spanked his bottom. I told him that what he did was bad, that he hurt his sister, and that he should never do it again. I said that he had to stay in his room until I told him that it would be all right to come downstairs again. Regina wasn't physically hurt. Her guardian angel was there to keep her safe. I hugged her and held her until she calmed down. When John came back downstairs, I made him tell Regina that he was sorry.

Along with his anger, another problem was developing. John started biting and tearing things apart such as clothing or papers. He even tried to bite me and others.

At this time, John was taking Phenobarbital as an anticonvulsant. In addition, Dr. Roberts added Thorazine, a medication which was meant to help control severe behavior problems. He reassured us that these medications would not interfere with each other.

Because of John's sudden outbursts, it became difficult for us to go to church, or anywhere else, as a family. Either my husband or I would stay at home with John.

CHAPTER
34

March was a better month for John. The medication seemed to be helping. There were fewer outbursts both at home and in school. Mr. Capisano sent home notes saying that John responded well many times and seemed to be in constant contact with his environment. One day, he did all of the puzzles that they had in school, asked for soda, and to go outside. He marched with the other children and even played ball with them. He was good at picture recognition, enjoyed playing with clay, making snakes and horses, and he knew the letters in his name. John enjoyed toy phones and was talkative when he was playing with them. At home, John was doing better as well. He was even more playful with Regina. However, John wanted constant attention. If he couldn't communicate about something which was on his mind or if he felt that he wasn't getting enough attention, that's when he would throw a tantrum and become disruptive. Sometimes he walked around, as if in a daze, and seemed to be very sleepy. He also spoke in whispers most of the time. By the end of March, both Mr. Capisano and I agreed that something was bothering John, but neither one of us could figure out what that "something" was.

There was a two-week spring break in April. During that time, John's behavior remained more or less the same; however, there were a couple of changes. John would not sit down. He stood up most of the day, and he also refused to eat. This continued into May. Little by little, he started to sit again, and little by little, he started to be more cooperative, playful, and responsive both at school and at home. However, he still refused to eat anything. Until the end of May, he only drank water and then decided to add chocolate ice cream to his menu.

We were at a loss as to what we could do about it. The school recommended that we schedule a visit with Dr. Smith who had worked with some of the other students as well. He prescribed Ritalin, one tablet a day. Ritalin is a stimulant which affects chemicals in the brain that contribute to hyperactivity and impulse control. The medication seemed to help John to be in a better mood. He also started eating soup along with his ice cream and eventually ate his lunch, working up to two peanut-butter-and-jelly sandwiches. John was also doing better in school. He was more in contact with his surroundings, responding more to directions, and was more conversational. Once he started eating meals regularly again, he wouldn't eat peanut butter and jelly anymore. He would just throw it in the garbage.

The remainder of the school year was pretty much the same as it had been. There were days when John was responsive and cooperative and days when he was quiet, disruptive, or uncooperative. At the end of the year, I received a final report from each of the staff who were involved in John's program. They all concluded that he did poorly at first, gradually improved until January when things went downhill, and then picked up again toward the end of the school year.

Mr. Capisano wrote us a letter on the last day of school which read:

> Since it is the last day of school, I now look back over the year to measure John's progress in various areas including academic, perception, behavior and self-care. It is difficult to measure such progress for John who has had his ups and downs in all of the above areas. Most of the staff have seen change, and indeed so have I. Personally, I think that John has more potential than I could have tapped. There was a period of three months when I was very concerned, but now he has begun to learn and follow more directions. His fears have somewhat diminished, while social contact has increased. I hope that I have in some

way helped your son. Thank you for your coop-
eration, patience and above all encouragement,
which has sustained me throughout the school
year.

Respectfully yours,
Mr. A. Capisano.

Although plans were being formulated for John to return to
At-The-Cliffs in September, this was to be our final correspondence.

When we met with Dr. Smith back in April, he recommended
that we see Dr. Rose Felman, who was a clinical psychologist associ-
ated with the National Institute For Children, in Media, PA. We sent
her a letter requesting an appointment for consultation and received
a response scheduling May 21, 1968, at 11:15 AM, to bring John in
for evaluation. We were to send her John's medical records pertaining
to any previous neurological studies, and the completed forms which
were attached to the letter regarding general information about John.
We accepted the appointment.

It was to be a two-day process. We were fortunate enough to
have one of my husband's Navy friends living in the area of the
Institute with his wife and son who happened to be the same age as
Regina. We made arrangements to stay with them overnight and they
agreed to take care of Regina when we took John for his evaluation
with Dr. Felman. Everything worked out very well.

There were many areas of testing involved in this evaluation
including psychological, social skills, language comprehension,
vocabulary, and motor skills. We didn't get the results of these evaluations until July. When it was done, Dr. Felman concluded that John
had a primary neurological problem with secondary retardation and
a severe emotional overlay. She said that any rehabilitation program
that might be considered should have emphasis on motor perceptual
skills, eye-hand coordination and control, language stimulation, and
organizational techniques.

Little did we know that this would be the beginning of events which would change our lives completely. In retrospect, this interruption of his routine could've been what had an effect on John's behavior since he couldn't express himself verbally. Unfortunately we will never know the answer to that.

CHAPTER

35

The summer of 1968 was the time for us to make the hardest decision of our lives. Should we continue to have John live at home with us? Or do we seriously accept the advice of the doctors that as John grew older and stronger, problems with his behavior would be harder for us to handle. Our social life as a family would continue to be affected, my husband would have to be more involved with John's personal hygiene, and John would only be able to learn as much as possible whatever he was taught in school. Would it be better for John, and for us, if he were to live in a place where he could learn to live and interact with his peers, not only in a school setting but in a home-like setting as well? People whose life's work is teaching and caring for individuals like John would more likely be able to deal with any and all of John's needs better than we could. It would definitely be very hard for John and for the three of us at home to adjust to this new life, but in the long run, would it be the best decision for the four of us? What to do?

In June, we got a letter from the Institute for Achievement of Human Potential in Pennsylvania. They had received a letter of referral from Dr. Roberts on behalf of John and could now proceed with a full evaluation of John and instructions for the family. The appointment was originally set for September 8 and 9 then changed to December 16 because of some changes to their program. It would be a five-day process including 2 days for evaluation, 2 days for parent orientation, and a final day for teaching the specific program for the child to the parents, after which we would return home to carry out the program. We would then be required to return every sixty or ninety days for re-evaluation and possible revisions. We were told that in order for them to set up a program especially for John, they would need complete background information on him. We were sent an eighteen-page questionnaire regarding John's history going back to day one, including past and present medical history, past and present medications, stages of development such as walking, talking, feeding, and dressing himself, etc. They required a record of any medical tests that were done or of any allergies or immunizations. This had to be returned on our first visit with John. We also had to sign forms for them to be able to contact any physician, hospital, or agency with which John had any contact and mail them back to the institute.

In the meantime, we were able to get more information regarding the institute's program which was at least, at the beginning, "patterning." The doctors at the institute concluded that children learned their best in stages and in order to progress, one of the first stages was to be able to crawl properly. Once achieved, the brain would be ready to proceed to the next stage of development. Patterning required five people for seven days a week to participate in the program. One person to work each arm, one person to work each leg, and one person at the head. The idea was to move each extremity in a proper crawling mode until it could be done by the child without help.

If you recall in an earlier chapter where crawling was introduced to John's program at school, not only didn't he like it but he was so uncooperative that they had to discontinue it. Besides the fact that it was discontinued from his program, we couldn't come up with enough names of people to contact who would be able to take on the commitment necessary to be part of John's patterning. We'd obviously need more than just five people in order to keep the program going for an extended period of time. Because of these reasons, we decided to write a letter to the institute and cancel our December date. Again the question—what to do?

CHAPTER

36

During the summer months, the Fair Lawn Board of Education was in the process of locating a residential placement for John. Mr. Miller was the person in charge. We went with him to visit three of them. The first was a New Jersey state school located in Woodbridge. The only thing that I remember about the place was that we walked into a large room which was rather dark where there were many residents just sitting around. Some were in wheelchairs, some were curled up on the floor, some walking aimlessly around. However, I don't remember seeing anyone supervising the residents or interacting with any of them. This place was definitely unacceptable. I don't know why Mr. Miller even bothered to take us there. Next we went to the North Jersey Training School located in Totowa. I don't remember anything about it except that it was a step-or-two above the first place. Then we went with Mr. Miller to a place called Springbrook, located in Oneonta, New York. This place was totally different from the other two. It was very bright, airy, and colorful as I remember it. There was an area set up like a Main Street with little shops and an ice-cream place. The purpose was to teach the residents how to shop and to use money. The living space was quite nice also, and the ratio of staff to resident was pretty good as well, but John was not to be accepted there either because he wasn't qualified or there was no opening at the time. Again I don't know why Mr. Miller even took us to see the place.

It all worked out well, however, because an opening became available at the Algonquin School located in Upstate New York. According to the Fair Lawn Board of Education, it had a great reputation and it was the best place in the state. It was a converted Victorian house which had only 19 residents with 5 staff members.

It was run by a husband and wife who were both educators. The only problem was that it was located in Saranac Lake, about 300 miles north in the Adirondack Mountains. Could we even think about John living so far away and that our visits with him would be extremely limited? Mr. Miller told us that we had to make a decision as soon as possible before someone else would take the opportunity away from us.

We made contact by phone with the directors, Mr. and Mrs. Knight. After speaking with them at great length, we were certain that John's placement at Algonquin was the right one. They answered all of our questions and took away any fears or apprehensions that we had. They reassured us that John would receive all of the care and attention that he would need, and they were also sure that after a period of adjustment, John would feel happy and secure. We told the board of education to go ahead with the arrangements.

CHAPTER

37

Neither my husband nor I can recall what the time was like between the end of the school year in June until December when we made the trip to Saranac Lake. We couldn't remember whether or not John went to school in September. Most likely he did not. We spent the summer doing as many things together as we could. We went to the zoo where John, for some reason or another loved to look at the donkeys. We went to Allaire State Park where they ran a steam-engine train which John loved to ride. We went to Memorial Pool which was a few blocks away from our house. We visited some of our friends and neighbors who related well to John and always made a fuss over him especially Josie and Frank. They really loved John, and he was always happy to see them. Josie used to have a Hershey bar in her pocketbook to give to John so every time that he would see her, he would say, "Hi, Jo. Candy," and go straight to her pocketbook. He would have to give her a kiss, however, before he got his candy.

We received a list from the Algonquin School of the things that John would need once he was living up there: so many pairs of socks, underwear, shirts, pants, sweaters, etc. We wanted to make sure that he had enough of everything to take with him, so we bought some new clothes for him. Then on December 3, Dr. Roberts saw John for the last time. He was pleased that we made the decision to place John in resident school. He talked to John a little, shook his hand, and wished him well. His final entry in John's medical record read, "60 lbs., 49 inches. No contagions. Thorazine and Mysolin still recommended. Satisfactory check-up. Algonquin School, NY State.". The question "What to do?" was finally answered.

CHAPTER

38

It was early morning on December 5, 1968, that the four of us got into our car, along with Johnny's things and our own overnight bags, and started on what was a very long, tiring, and tense ride to Saranac Lake, New York. We stopped a few times to stretch our legs, get some food, and use the restrooms. The weather was pretty good at first but the farther north we got, the colder it got as well. The clouds got heavier too. We were in the mountain area and when we got off of the Northway onto a two-lane highway, it started to snow. One of our headlights decided to conk out on us. Eventually the snow got so heavy and the visibility so bad that we could hardly see the road ahead of us. It had gotten dark, and we couldn't really tell where we were. We just kept moving slowly and praying, "God help us!" He did! We could barely see it, but there it was, two red lights on the back of a car! Keeping a safe distance, we followed that car hoping that it was going where we were going. Finally we saw a sign, "Lake Placid." There were streetlights and road signs, and we were able to find our way to the motel where we would be staying overnight. Thank God we got there safely. During the night, the snow stopped and the sun was shining brightly. The snowplows had come through town. After breakfast, we were able to make our way to Saranac Lake which was about ten miles west from where we were.

Mr. and Mrs. Knight were there to greet us along with a staff person who helped care for the residents. Unfortunately I don't remember her name, but I can still see her face. She was an older woman with a pleasant smile, and she greeted us, especially Johnny, in a caring way. It was a very warm welcome. The place was charming and clean and looked like home. We didn't stay very long, but the Knights did reassure us that Johnny would be fine once he made an adjustment to his new home and everyone there got adjusted to him. They told us that they would prefer we didn't contact them but that they would contact us once he settled in. We knew that it would be hard for us but that it was in Johnny's best interest. They also mentioned that they would take Johnny off of the behavior medications which he was taking because they believed that loving care and redirection was a better way to control bad behaviors. That was music to my ears!

The time came for parting. As I write, I can still feel the emotions welling up inside me and the tears starting to accumulate. "Dear God, are we making a mistake? How can I say goodbye to my son and leave him here with strangers so far from our home? How can I explain to him the 'why' of it all? How can I tell him that we won't be seeing him for a long time but that we would be back to visit when we can?" I knew that we had to go, so I tried my best to explain it to him, gave him a big hug and a kiss, said goodbye, then turned around, and went out the door. My husband and Regina said goodbye in their own way. When we got into the car, drove down the driveway and away from the school, which was now our son's home, we stopped the car and cried our hearts out.

Once we got going, we saw the road which we had driven on getting up to Lake Placid the night before. There were so many turns, most of which were along cliffs with no barriers. We knew for sure that it was God who gave us the way safely to our destination. We drove as far as Lake George where we stopped for lunch. We were able to relax a little and talk about how we felt, and then we got into the car and made our way back home to Fair Lawn.

CHAPTER 39

Things would be different without Johnny. We knew that from the minute we woke up the next morning. The house seemed exceptionally quiet and empty as if no one was at home. It was Sunday. We had our breakfast and went to Mass. We spent the rest of the day trying to escape from the reality that Johnny was no longer with us. John did some reading. I played a little with Regina, and then she kept herself busy with her toys and dolls. After lunch, we watched television together, and then I went upstairs to Johnny's room and just sat there for a while, thinking about how much I missed him. I started to put his clothes and things all together in one place. I knew that eventually, they would all go up to Johnny's new home. Before I knew it, it was time to cook dinner. We only had a few more hours to go and the day would be over.

Monday came and after breakfast, John went to work. Except for the fact that my thoughts kept wondering if Johnny was having any problems adjusting to his new home, life went on as usual. We hoped that soon we would hear from the Knights telling us that he was doing well. We had our own adjustments to make. The most difficult thing I had to do was to let go of the guilt I felt having to place Johnny in a residence school, one which was so far from home. Regina had questions. Where was Johnny? Isn't he coming home? Why not? The one that broke my heart was, "Will I have to go away too?"

A short time passed when I noticed that Regina's behavior began to change. It was as though she wanted more attention. However, that couldn't be it because she was getting more attention than she had ever gotten before. I was able to get in touch with the child psychologist who worked in the Fair Lawn school system, and

I explained the situation to her. She agreed to come to our home. When Mrs. B came to visit, she spoke with Regina, played games with her, and asked her some questions. She said that after her evaluation was done, we would hear from her. After a few days, Mrs. B got in touch with us. We met with her, and this is what she concluded. Regina was trying to make up for the lack of tension which she lived with from the time she was an infant. It all made sense. Mrs. B gave us suggestions as to how to deal with it and in a short time, Regina's behavior was back to normal.

At last! We received a letter from Mr. Knight. I could hardly wait to open it. The first sentence read, "We are happy to say that Johnny is getting along fine now." Apparently he wasn't sleeping or eating well at first, but the last sentence read, "We do not think there will be any further trouble with Johnny, and that he has accepted his new home and environment. He is well liked by all, and we look forward to working with him. Sincerely yours."

With a sigh of relief and some tears of joy, I could now let go of my guilty feelings.

CHAPTER 40

As the days passed, we found that we had more time to do things as a family. We could go to a restaurant, a movie, a visit with friends or relatives, or any other place without concern for unexpected behavior to upset our plans. We were able to spend time doing whatever we wanted to do including just relaxing or doing nothing at all.

Christmas was just a couple of weeks away. We got busy decorating the house, outside and inside, putting up a tree with all the trimmings, and last-minute shopping for stocking stuffers. We had already bought gifts for Johnny and brought them with us when we took him up to Saranac Lake.

Looking forward to Christmas Day was always exciting. It was a little different this time, but we were ready to celebrate the birth of our Savior.

Christmas Eve was spent at Mom and Dad's house in Brooklyn with aunts, uncles, and cousins. Twenty-three of us for a traditional Italian meal which included antipasto, spaghetti with clam sauce, other traditional fish dishes, fruit, nuts and desserts. Then after dinner, we'd open our presents. On the way home, we passed some very high apartment buildings which had red beacon lights on the rooftops. They were there to guide airplanes to the runways at the nearby airport. We used to tell Johnny and Regina that the red light was Rudolph's nose guiding the other reindeer and Santa's sleigh. They would spot the red lights until they fell asleep. We always enjoyed Christmas Eve with my husband's family.

On Christmas Day, after all of the gifts were opened, we would sing Happy Birthday to Jesus, have breakfast and go to Mass. The church was decorated with wreaths, garland, poinsettia plants, and a big beautiful tree. There was a life-sized nativity scene on the side of the altar. The people all seemed happier, wishing everyone a "Merry Christmas." The music was uplifting, and all of the people sang out. It was a great way to start the day.

We spent the rest of the day with my Mom and Dad but not in the Bronx. My brother Rudy had a house way out in Long Island, about two hours away. My brother Richie would drive his family and Mom and Dad there, and we spent the day together. More gifts to open, and of course, there would be another big meal. Pasta, meatballs, sausage and braciola, followed by turkey with all the trimmings, fruit, and dessert. After spending another day with family, we headed home, and it took a couple of days before we got back to a normal routine. Although we spent Christmas 1968 without Johnny's presence, he was there in our hearts. As for me, most of my thoughts were 300 miles north.

CHAPTER

41

In the first week of January, we received a letter from Mr. Knight, dated December 31, 1968. The letter was long, and the news was good. He wrote that Johnny enjoyed Christmas. He had lots of presents and seemed interested in everything that was going on. They placed a small Christmas tree in every room, and Johnny especially liked helping to trim the trees. This was something he had never done before. The children received their stockings on Christmas Eve and on Christmas Day, they found their presents piled under the tree in their room. Johnny had a good time opening every one of them. He also wrote that Johnny seemed to be quite content and cooperative. No more crying. No more asking to go with his parents. Those words were good to know but were also a little bittersweet. We received a letter just about every month with an update on Johnny's progress and about all of the things that the children were doing.

February was a very busy month for them. They celebrated with several birthday parties including one for Lincoln and Washington and a Valentine's party as well. Johnny enjoyed all of them and "ate ice cream until it came out of his ears." He had been very well-behaved and getting along with everyone. He was no longer on any tranquillizers, and he was doing well and sleeping much better. There was a lot more snow than usual in Saranac Lake that month, and the children enjoyed tobogganing and snow sculpting. It was good to know that Johnny was content and doing so well. The March letter was equally positive, and I wrote a response to Mr. Knight to let him know how pleased we were to receive his letters and to learn about the progress Johnny was making each month.

Johnny's birthday was coming up on April 22. Mr. Knight asked us to send him a basketball and a sleeping bag. It was a pleasure for me to be buying something like that for him instead of the usual puzzles, coloring books, and toys. The children had a point system which enabled them to accumulate points for doing certain chores and following certain rules like putting a chair back in place when you got up after a meal or clearing your place at the table, etc. When they had enough points, they could then buy a toy for themselves. This taught them responsibility and handling small amounts of money.

I expressed our gratitude for the dedication, concern, and love that was shown for the children attending their school and the comfort that it gave us. We also let Mr. Knight know that we were planning a visit to see Johnny. We had considered going up for his birthday, but we weren't able to make it before the first Friday in May. Our plans were to pick Johnny up on Saturday morning after breakfast and take him out to spend the rest of the day with us. We wished them a blessed Easter and wrote that we were looking forward to our visit and to making our trip up to Saranac Lake, this time, without a snow storm.

CHAPTER 42

Time passed and on Easter morning, Regina's basket was waiting for her on the kitchen table. She was excited and could hardly wait to tear it open and start eating the candy. We told her that she could only have one piece before breakfast. With a big smile on her face, Regina found the biggest piece, aside from the chocolate bunny, and ate it. After breakfast, we got dressed and went to church but not before Regina ate another piece of candy.

Easter Mass was always very festive. Almost everyone had on a new Easter outfit. Easter lilies were everywhere along with other beautiful spring flowers. The music was uplifting, and everyone seemed joyful. The only thing missing was Johnny. As soon as we got back home, we telephoned Algonquin. Mrs. Knight answered the phone, and we spoke for a few minutes. She told us that each of the residents found an Easter basket in their room, and they dug right in. Johnny was no exception. He loved candy. Then they all enjoyed breakfast and a visit from the Easter Bunny.

We told Mrs. Knight that we wanted to speak to Johnny, so she brought him to the phone. We said, "Hi, Johnny. Happy Easter!"

He said, "Happy Easter!" I asked him if he liked his Easter basket, and he said, "Candy." I asked him if he saw the Easter Bunny, and he said, "Bunny!" Then he said, "Goodbye," and left the phone. Mrs. Knight said that Johnny had gone back with the other children, and we ended the conversation. It was obvious, Johnny didn't like talking on the phone.

Two weeks later after John got home from work, we telephoned Algonquin again to wish Johnny a happy birthday. Mr. Knight told us that Johnny had a good day and that they had a birthday party for him that afternoon. After blowing out the candles and singing

"Happy Birthday," there was cake and ice cream. As usual, Johnny devoured his share and more, and he had a big smile on his face as he tore open his presents. He enjoyed being the center of attention. Mr. Knight said that they would make good use of the basketball and sleeping bag along with the other things we sent him. Then Johnny came to the phone and we sang "Happy Birthday" to him. Our conversation followed. "Did you have a birthday party today?"

Answer, "Party."

"Do you like your presents?"

Answer, "Presents."

"Did you have a fun day today?"

Answer, "Fun."

Then we said, "We love you, and we're coming to visit you soon."

Answer, "See ya."

The next voice was Mr. Knight who told us that Johnny left the phone and went back with the other children. Apparently he'd had enough phone talk. We confirmed our visit, which we were looking forward to in less than two weeks, then said goodbye and ended the conversation.

CHAPTER
43

Time went by quickly, and the day came for us to visit Johnny. It was the beginning of May, a beautiful day with no threats of snow! We left after breakfast to begin our long drive to Saranac Lake. We actually didn't mind the trip much once we got past the local traffic and on to the highways. We stopped every couple of hours to stretch our legs and to eat lunch and dinner. In between, we sang songs and played car games. We enjoyed the beautiful scenery especially in the mountains. Everything was either already in bloom or beginning to bloom. We got to Lake Placid, checked in to the motel, and were ready for a good night's sleep. We woke up to another beautiful, sunny day, had breakfast, and were on our way. We phoned the Knights to let them know what time we'd pick up Johnny and asked that they pack a bathing suit. The motel had a heated, indoor pool, and we planned on spending some time there with Johnny and Regina.

We had only a few more miles to get to Saranac Lake and to seeing our son after five long months. I couldn't wait to see him again, but I was getting a little nervous. Thoughts were racing through my mind. What kind of greeting would we get? Would he be happy to see us or angry because we left him there? What kind of reaction would there be when we brought him back again after spending the day with us? I'd know the answers soon enough because we were driving up the long driveway to the house, and I saw Johnny waiting at the big picture window in the front room.

We got to the door, and Mr. and Mrs. Knight were there to greet us. They said that Johnny was at the window most of the morning, watching for us and waiting to go. They brought us in to the front room, and Johnny was standing there with a big smile on his face. He walked up to Regina and looked at her, and she said, "Hi, Johnny!"

He smiled and then went next to my husband who gave him a big hug and said, "Hi, Johnny! I'm so happy to see you again."

Finally he got to me, looked me straight in the eyes, and before I could say anything, he gave me a very hard slap across my face! I was stunned and so was everybody else. Before anyone would reprimand him, however, I grabbed him and hugged him tight and said, "I'm sorry, son. I love you!" In that moment, I knew why he slapped me, and I couldn't blame him. I broke the promise which I made to him that I would never leave him, and he remembered that promise. I cannot forget the slap which hurt physically, yes, but most of all emotionally. The Knights felt terrible and apologized, but it wasn't their fault. I had betrayed Johnny who trusted me. He was prompted to tell me that he was sorry which he did. I hugged him again, and he smiled at me. It was all over. We left the house, went back to the motel, and enjoyed the rest of the day.

We went out for lunch. We talked and spent most of the time having fun at the pool in the motel. Both Johnny and Regina loved being in the water, especially Regina. She would jump right in whether or not the water was cold. She'd come out, run around to the side, and jump in again. Johnny was much more cautious. He walked down the steps holding on to Dad. However, I noticed that he was watching Regina and after a while, he got out of the pool and decided to give it a try. He made sure that Dad was there to catch him, took the chance, and jumped in. That was a milestone for Johnny, and we cheered and clapped for him. Before we knew it, the time came to bring him back home.

We told the Knights about our day and when they asked Johnny if he had fun, he answered, "Fun." With lots of hugs and kisses, we said goodbye to Johnny and told him that we would come back again to visit. A staff person came to get him and brought him back to the other children. After he had gone, we talked a few minutes with Mr. and Mrs. Knight and then said our goodbyes and left. We went to have some dinner then back to the motel. The next morning, we left Lake Placid and made our way back home to Fair Lawn. All was well. Questions were answered, and I knew that the next time we would visit Johnny, things would be easier.

CHAPTER 44

Shortly after our visit, Mr. Knight informed us that the children were taken to a musical concert. They all behaved so well that the conductor told them that he wished more children would come and behave as nicely as they did. "It made us proud to hear that." Mr. Knight also mentioned that Johnny enjoyed being outdoors, especially picnics. He made use of the playground equipment and participated in nature studies. When the weather got warmer, Johnny liked to play in the water. At first, he only got his feet wet, but eventually with help he attempted to swim by himself. The summer went by and school started again. Mr. Knight informed us that his married daughter Glenda, and her husband Ray, had joined the staff. Glenda had a Master's Degree in special education and would be working a great deal with Johnny.

The next big event in Johnny's life was the Halloween party. The children all enjoyed making many decorations including decorating the food. Glenda wrote that she thought she'd never have to feed Johnny again but of course, the next morning he was hungry again. They all wore costumes, played games, and had a lot of fun. In school, Johnny was much more responsive and was able to do everything that was asked of him. When winter came, he enjoyed playing both indoors and outdoors and continued to show more interest in school.

In November, as usual, a special meal was prepared for Thanksgiving Day; and in December, the excitement and preparations for Christmas began. Of course, Santa would be coming, and there would be presents for everyone. Early in January, Glenda decided that since Johnny was growing up and doing so well, the time had come for him to be referred to as John. We totally agreed, and Johnny adjusted to the change to his name right away.

In February, the children once again had their share of parties. First there was Lincoln's birthday and then Valentine's day with cake and games and receiving Valentine cards. For Washington's birthday, the children helped to decorate the dining room in red, white, and blue. After dinner, there was a special cake decorated with a cherry tree, and they sang, "Happy Birthday" to George Washington. Following that, they had a talent show where John got up and sang a short song for the group. In March, the children celebrated St. Patrick's Day. They all wore green hats and enjoyed the festivities. Easter came along in April with special decorations, Easter baskets and a birthday party for John. More cake and candy, and of course presents. In May, the children walked into town for the Memorial Day parade and ceremonies. They each received a small flag to wave in the air, enjoyed the music and seeing the soldiers marching. In the last week of June, the children were taken on a trip to Santa's workshop. They took a picnic lunch with them. There were reindeer to feed and pet, a magic show, a nativity pageant, and, of course, Santa. There was also a train ride which went under waterfalls and through tunnels. John really enjoyed that. At the end of the day, everyone was tired and happy to be going back home. In July, the children enjoyed their first hotdog and marshmallow roast in the backyard. John and the others had to find their own stick and then roast their own food over the grill. It was such a big hit that another one was planned before the summer was over. John had been working on a key chain that summer. He had to sand a small piece of wood, paint it, glue a picture on it, and varnish it. He completed it with some help from Glenda. School started again in the fall, and John seemed to be more attentive in class. As time went on, he became more active and seemed happier.

CHAPTER
45

John lived at the Algonquin school for eight years. During that time, he learned a lot and accomplished a lot as well. He learned to identify things and could connect them such as a ball with a bat, a sock with a shoe, etc. He could identify colors and use them correctly such as a yellow banana, a red apple, a brown dog, and the like. John could pick out the letters of his name from the other letters and with guidance, he began to draw them. He never quite mastered it, but he did get better at it. I remember the first time I received a Mother's Day card from him which, with some help, he colored in a rose and wrote the letters of his name at the bottom. It made me feel very happy and proud. Every Easter, the children enjoyed Easter egg hunts, bunny races, and imitating games. John got the booby prize one year for his imitation of a chick which sounded more like a cow and looked like a duck with arthritis. He got lots of attention and enjoyed the prize. John also did much better during walks of some distance.

Things were planned one thing after another. As John became more acclimated to the winter weather, he enjoyed being outside with the other children especially sledding down the hill. Just before Christmas, the children put on a nativity pageant. Several Girl Scout troops, a business club from the Saranac Lake High School, and a group from a nearby rehabilitation center attended the performance. Of course, there was a party afterward. The local newspaper printed a picture of the children along with a short article in their next edition. Every year, John enjoyed the excitement of Christmas and was always the first one to greet Santa and stand by his side waiting for his present. Afterward, he helped to pick up the wrappings. There were sledding parties with other schools, and John really enjoyed going down the hill. There were dance classes, gymnastics, and basketball classes, all of which kept the children busy. They were also learning how to handle money and were given a weekly job to do. We were asked to send John an allowance so that he would have his own money to spend for McDonald's, movies, and other things. In 1976, Algonquin entered the Special Olympics, and John took first place in softball throw! The school entered a float in the winter carnival. The theme was The *Little Old Woman Who Lived in a Shoe*, and all of the children took part in the parade. They also entered a snow sculpture and won first place!

CHAPTER
46

The following summer, the boys and girls completed an overnight camping trip which proved to be one of the best learning experiences for them. Prior to the trip, each of the students was assigned jobs to do, different from those at the school. They had to carry their own sleeping bag and canteen. They also had to learn how to get in and out of the sleeping bag and how to roll it up again. They learned how to use a flashlight, to help with collecting wood for the fire, and with cooking, cleanup, and other tasks which were necessary for a campout.

The boys went first. Along with staff people, they drove to the Adirondack Lodge at Mount Marcy where they met up with a Boy Scout troop. A newspaper reporter was at the Lodge. He interviewed them and also got a story about the school's sports program. From there, the boys completed the hike. However, along the way, they had to work their way around a very large mud hole and at one point, they had to walk on some logs which wasn't very easy for them. They finally arrived at the place where they set up the tent and gathered wood for the fire. Mr. Ray, Glenda's husband, started the fire over which hamburger stew was cooked and marshmallows roasted. When it was time for bed, the boys were quite tired, but John "kept the wild beasts away with his noises during the night." They woke up early in the morning to pancakes for breakfast and got everything geared up and ready for the hike back down where Glenda met them for the ride back home. Glenda said that it was a goldmine of learning and fun for everyone regardless of their age or capabilities.

Unfortunately there was an incident which wasn't fun at all. It happened one day when I woke up with an eerie feeling that something was going to go wrong. However, the day went by and everything seemed all right. Then after dinner, we received a phone call from Glenda. She told us that John had an accident. The students were outside playing, and John walked in front of one of them who was on a swing. The swing hit John in the face. His nose bled and his mouth and chin as well. His two front teeth broke, one slightly and the other in half. He was taken to the hospital where he was treated and sent home. It would take a few days for the swelling to go down, and he'd have to eat soft food, but thank God his nose was not broken and his eyes were not affected. A few years later, the two front teeth had to come out, but it never interfered with his beautiful smile or his ability to eat well.

CHAPTER

47

It was a sad day in April 1976 when we received a letter from Glenda informing us that on March 26, the school suffered an extensive fire. The students and staff were evacuated without injuries. All three stories of the north wing of the school had severe structural damage. Upon investigation by the deputy commissioner of the Department of Mental Hygiene, it was advised that in order to continue operation of the school, regulations, which had been recently enacted, required that a completely new structure be erected. No other alternatives were given. Therefore, because it would've been impossible for them to meet the cost for such a project, as of August 1, 1976, the Algonquin School would have to be closed. Until the closing date, they were to be housed in the gymnasium of a nearby college which would still be closed for the summer. New placements would have to be made for each of the students, and Glenda said that she would do everything possible to help with making the appropriate placement for them. As a group, the students were told that they would all be going to a new school. They were able to ask questions and talk about it. The staff did their best to make it sound exciting to be going to a new school. Glenda closed her letter with the following:

> Over the past six years, I have enjoyed my work and the relationship with my students. I will miss them terribly. Yet, I feel that in these six years each student has progressed and become a more self-sufficient individual. I am very proud to have guided them in this direction.

A "graduation" was held at the end of May at the college with a buffet following. Parents were invited to attend; but unfortunately, my husband and I were not able to make the long trip at that time.

After the initial shock, the thoughts, concerns, and questions began flooding our minds. We could only imagine what Glenda and her staff were going through. We thought about the students having to leave everything behind and moving from the school to the gymnasium and then on to another place. The first questions we had were: what happens now? How will it affect John? How will it affect us? We knew that Algonquin had been the best placement possible and that he had done so well there, but what would the next place be like for him? We knew that we had to spend a lot of time in prayer and to put our faith and trust in God who always knows what's best and works all things together for good. We also decided to ask our friends to pray as well, and they were happy to do so.

One of our friends, Charlie, was planning to run in the New York City marathon and said that he would do it for John. This marathon is over twenty-six miles long. It runs through all five boroughs of NYC and takes an average of about five hours to complete. It requires lots of training but nevertheless, the runners still experience exhaustion and pain. While running, they must remain hydrated because they will lose about 5 pounds of perspiration. It definitely wasn't going to be easy for Charlie, but he did it. He said that every time he felt a pain or wanted to quit, he remembered John, said a prayer, and kept on going. We knew that Charlie's gift would not go unnoticed by God.

My husband and I talked about our feelings and concerns and then decided to telephone Glenda. We didn't bombard her with questions because we knew that she wouldn't have the answers, but we wanted her to know how truly saddened we were when we read her letter regarding the closing of the school, and also that we knew Glenda would do everything possible to make the proper placements for the students. We told her how pleased we were with the progress John had made while living at Algonquin and that we would miss the relationship which we had with her over the years. We spoke a little about the fire. Glenda said that they were able to salvage some of the clothing, toys, and belongings of the students but that most of it was destroyed. We were able to keep in touch with her until things were finalized. My husband and I knew that it would be difficult to find another place like the Algonquin School. Saying goodbye was very hard for all concerned.

CHAPTER
48

On July 2, 1976, three months after the fire at Algonquin School, John began the next phase of his life at the Keystone Residence and Camp in Gouldsboro, Pennsylvania. This was the same place that found John unacceptable in August 1968 based on the fact that he would definitely need one-on-one supervision. During that space of time, however, Keystone had expanded their program, and John had made more progress. Keystone was a very lovely place. There were many acres of land which were nicely landscaped. It was park-like with several benches and picnic tables in various places. There was an office building with areas for activities and other buildings for living quarters. John shared a room with six other boys. Everything was clean and well-maintained. School, however, was in the public-school system off premises, and the residents were transported back and forth each day. As lovely as it was, it couldn't compare with the home-like atmosphere that he was used to at Algonquin.

Upon admission, the administrator, Mrs. Lozzi, sent a letter to the Department of Institutions and Agencies in New Jersey with a copy to us in which she made note that upon John's entrance to Keystone, a psychological examination portrayed a boy in a very confused state. He was described as very restless, having an extremely limited attention span, and was self-abusive. He wanted the counselors' full attention and asked them for kisses. "Of course," she quoted, "he's too big a boy for this type of attention." Mrs. Lozzi's opinion was that John would probably not fit in to their program but that they would be willing to give him a sixty-day trial period starting September 1, hoping that John would prove them wrong. As you will see, John stayed on.

CHAPTER
49

In the year between John's admission to Keystone and the following year, John's evaluation made it obvious that he had become "more of a person" and was beginning to enjoy life. In her letter to the supervisor at the Department of Institutions and Agencies, Ms. Lozzi stated that she was hopeful of being able to draw a great deal more potential out of John but that it would be a slow process. She also said that "he is affectionate and lovable, enjoys attention and responds to a great many staff members. This is an asset which I hope to utilize for future development."

Some of the observations made in the evaluation process were as follows (notice that most things had already been accomplished at Algonquin):

"John will do any little thing for attention which he seems to crave most of the time. He can be silly and also displays a sense of humor. John enjoys sports and recreational activities but needs encouragement to participate. He is slow to get started, but once started, he seems to enjoy himself. He shares a room with six other boys and gets along well with them. John is basically lazy and has to be coaxed even to pick up his slippers. He does take pleasure, however, in clearing off the table in the dining room and tries to eat the leftovers. At the table, John's eating habits are poor but when corrected, he usually responds. He is well-behaved most times. He manages most dressing skills without assistance. He can name and locate the parts of his body. John can throw and catch a ball, jumps, and kicks. He can match the basic shapes, can manipulate pegs and stack blocks, string beads, and reconstruct puzzles. John knows his name, can recognize it in print and is working on spelling his name using individual letter cards. John can count to five and match numbers

1–6. He is working on matching and sorting objects and will soon begin bagging them. He is not a behavior problem in the classroom. John will participate in various activities but needs constant prodding and prefers to go off by himself during recreation and free time.

Psychological testing classified John as severely retarded with a seizure disorder. He receives Mysoline 250 mgs and Phenobarbital 1½ gms at bedtime to control seizures although he has had none since admission. He also receives Mellaril 25 mgs three times a day to control self-abusive habits such as slapping himself and biting the skin around his fingernails. John is a rather interesting person to listen to when answering questions. He favors older staff members over the younger ones, and he greets them with a smile especially those he seems to respond to best.

On admission, John was very withdrawn and self-abusive. These areas have improved. He needs help to improve his daily living and communication skills, and to become involved more socially. John definitely has potential, likes to be helpful, and seems to have interest in work situations. Continued present placement is recommended."

And so, it was, that John continued life at Keystone.

One of the advantages of having John living there was the fact that it took us only about two hours to get to Gouldsboro from Fair Lawn. This made it possible for us to visit him often. Also, home visits were encouraged over holidays and for vacations. We didn't think it would be a good idea to bring John home for a visit and then have to bring him back again to Keystone until he got used to the place. We didn't even consider it during his first year there. However, in February 1977, we had a visit from Sister Ludavine who was assigned to our church in order to take a census and to find out if any of the parishioners had a special need. In the course of our conversation, I mentioned that our son had received his first Communion but not Confirmation. Sister didn't think that there would be any problem for him to receive Confirmation and suggested that we get in touch with our bishop. It just so happened that a new bishop had recently been assigned to our area. His name was Bishop Robert Garner. When he came to visit our church for the first time, he said that if he could be of help to anyone to let him know. We were to call his office and make an appointment to discuss it and that he would be happy to do whatever he could to help in any way. I phoned him and made an appointment.

When my husband and I met with Bishop Garner, we told him all about John and our desire for him to receive Confirmation. He was most gracious and told us that in April, he was scheduled to come to our parish in order to confirm those who had been preparing for it and that if we could bring John at that time, he would confirm him. He also said that because it would be difficult for him to sit through the whole Mass and ceremony, he would confirm John separately before Mass started. Much to the surprise of our pastor who was sure that I misunderstood the bishop, on April 24, 1977, Bishop Garner showed up early, and John was confirmed along with two other children in the parish for whom we got permission to include. A boy who like John had developmental disabilities, and a girl who because of serious back surgery was in a full body cast. They too weren't able to attend the Mass. John needed a sponsor for this occasion, and Frank, who John loved so much, agreed to sponsor him. Needless to say, it was a great day for celebration, and we were most grateful for Bishop Garner who made it possible.

John and his sponsor on Confirmation day

John stayed overnight with us, enjoyed the visit, and seemed happy to see Regina again. I cooked his favorite meal, pasta and meatballs with apple pie for dessert, which he devoured and asked for more. After the third helping, I had to tell him that there was no more. It reminded me of the time when we first brought him home and he ate nonstop. When we finished dinner, John helped us to clear the table. I don't remember how we passed the time, but I do remember singing to him. The song "You Light Up My Life" was very popular at the time, and I told John that it was his song because he was the one who lit up my life. From that time on, whenever I sang that song to him, he would smile. He even joined in with some of the words. When bedtime came, we told John that after breakfast we would be taking him back to Keystone, that everyone would be waiting for him, and that he could come again for another visit. He seemed to understand and accept it.

The next morning after breakfast, the three of us drove John back to Keystone. We spent some time with him and then said good-bye. We made our way home to Fair Lawn, thanking God that all went well.

CHAPTER
51

In the summer months that followed, the residents spent most of their time outdoors playing games, swimming, going on field trips, carnivals, and various other activities. John enjoyed the outdoors and especially being in the water. On July 30, the residents were guests at the big Parade of Champions which was a marching competition held at the Scranton Memorial Stadium. On July Fourth, they attended a spectacular firework display also held at the stadium.

Remember the physician who said that John had a sense of humor? Well, I can give you examples of that which took place on two of our visits to Keystone that summer. The first one was at a special event on July 31 when the residents put on the show *The Sound of Music*. I sang those songs together with John many times; and even though he couldn't sing all of the words, he certainly knew the melodies. However, John was not included in the show. Afterwards when I asked Mrs. Lozzi how come, she said that John didn't want to learn any of the songs. I told her to come with me. I took John by the hand, sat down with him, and said, "Come on, John, sing with me." We sang "Do, Re, Me," and Mrs. Lozzi was amazed. When she asked him why he wouldn't sing with the others, he just laughed and laughed. He had put one over on her. Following the show that day, a barbecue was held, and we all dug in and had a good time.

The second example came about when we received a phone call from Mrs. Lozzi, telling us that John was limping. The doctor had examined him but could find no reason for the limp. However, she wanted us to know that he would have someone walk with him in order to make sure that he wouldn't fall or get hurt. My husband John, Regina and I, decided to make a visit to Keystone and as she said, John was limping along. We assured her that we would take care of him and that he'd be all right. We walked a little and then decided to sit on one of the benches along the path. After a couple of minutes, I noticed another resident who was also limping and had an assistant walking with him. When I saw that, I turned to John and said, "I know why you're limping! You want attention. Am I right?" John laughed and laughed. I said, "Come on, let's go." There was no more limping. When we saw Mrs. Lozzi, I told her all about it. John laughed some more. Once again, he had put one over on her and the doctor and also tried to put one over on us, but I caught him! Summer was passing and soon, it would be time for school to begin again.

CHAPTER
52

Things seemed to be going well for John. He was approved by the State Department of Education to continue residence at Keystone for the 1978–'79 school year. As a result of his evaluation in October 1977, many goals were set for him to work on during that school year, mostly dealing with language and social skills. The evaluation showed that John had some improvement in gross motor skills and an increase in his attention span. However, he still needed assistance with buttons and tying his shoes which would be one of the goals in self-help skills. They also planned to develop fine motor skills, basic math concepts, printing skills, art, music, and physical education. The evaluation showed that John had adequate safety skills in following directions using stairways and hallways during fire drills. He was able to follow class rules, accept criticism, return objects after being used, follow directions of authority figures, accept blame for wrongdoing, and adjust his behavior to fit different situations. John could dust, vacuum, clean up spills, and throw trash in a proper receptacle.

We were sent a copy of the goals and how they would accomplish 75 percent to 100 percent of them by the end of the school year. It seemed like an impossible task to me, but I hoped that they would be able to do it.

CHAPTER
53

Before we knew it, the holidays were approaching. We decided to bring John home on Thanksgiving Day with an overnight stay. I informed Ms. Lozzi as to when John would be picked up and brought back again. We invited our parents who hadn't seen John in quite a while. I also invited my brother, Richie, and his family. He would drive my parents, who lived in the apartment building next-door to them. Mom and Dad Artale would be driving in from Brooklyn.

I prepared our traditional Thanksgiving meal of turkey, stuffing, sweet potatoes, mashed potatoes, stuffed mushrooms, and green bean casserole with nuts, fruit, pumpkin and apple pie for dessert. Everyone was happy to see John, and there were hugs, kisses, and smiles all around. Having the family together turned out to be a good idea. John was well-behaved, and it was a good visit. However, when it was dinner time, John didn't seem to want to eat. He kept looking around, so I asked him what he wanted. He said, "Pasta and meatballs."

Luckily I had cooked it earlier that week and had it in the freezer, so I said, "If that's what you want, I'll make it for you." I got it out, put it in the microwave, and John had his pasta and meatballs. Then he also ate some turkey and his favorite apple pie for dessert. After a good night's sleep, we drove John back to Keystone, and he accepted returning there very well.

Several parties and activities were scheduled at Keystone during the month of December, sponsored by different schools and churches in the area. There would be gifts, toys and treats for all, and Santa of course. John remained at Keystone for Christmas along with other residents who were not going to be away for the holiday. We sent him gifts, and the staff reassured us that they would provide a merry Christmas for all of them.

CHAPTER
54

We received a letter from John dated January 16, 1979. It was written by a staff person who obviously worked with him. Here's what it said:

> I'm being a good boy. When I go to school I play with the kids and I learn to count numbers, draw pictures and have fun. It's really snowing hard here and I have fun going out in the snow and sleigh riding with the rest of the kids. I'm doing fine and I like it here. We do a lot of activities. We color, play games, puzzles and musical games. I have six other boys in my room. We're all friends. I hope to see you soon.
>
> Love, John.

Even though we knew that John didn't write the letter himself, we were grateful that the staff person spent the time to write it for him. It meant a lot to us, and I've kept it all these years.

It seemed to us that things were going rather well for John. However, one month later, February 15, we received a phone call from Mrs. Lozzi telling us that John had been exhibiting extremely disruptive behavior and was very difficult to control. That day on a trip to Scranton with a couple of the other residents, John broke away from them, threw himself into a plate glass window of a store, and then ran out into the traffic. One of the staff people who was with them caught up with John and rushed him right back to Keystone. He wasn't injured but because of the incident, Mrs. Lozzi had him sent to the Clarks-Summit Psychiatric Hospital. She was sorry to give us that news, but there was no other alternative.

Needless to say, we were very upset and also kind of surprised. When I asked Mrs. Lozzi what happened to have caused such a drastic change within a month's time, she had no answer. There was nothing more that she could tell us. I asked her for the phone number of the hospital which she gave me, and the conversation ended.

Following the phone call, I remember crying and asking God, "What now?" When my husband finally calmed me down, my first words were, "Thank God that he wasn't hurt. He could've been hit by a car or cut by the glass window. He's probably confused, frightened, and who knows what else?" When he finally calmed me down, my husband reminded me that God was in charge and that everything would work out in His time and plan. It was hard for me to swallow what John said, but I knew that he was right. Okay, God's in charge, so again I asked, "What now?" The answer to that question was, "Pray!"

CHAPTER 55

As usual, praying brought some consolation. The first thought which God put into my mind was from the book of the prophet Habakkuk in the Holy Bible which read:

> The Lord answered me and said; Write down the vision clearly upon the tablets, so that one can read it readily. For the vision still has its time, presses on to fulfillment, and will not disappoint; if it delays, wait for it, it will surely come, it will not be late.

The vision I prayed for was that John would be placed in a residence where he would be happy and well-cared for. I thanked God for the answer, but little did I know then that it would be quite a while before that vision would come to fulfillment.

The second thought that came to me was to ask other people to pray for John as well. I called a friend who said that she would be happy to pray for John. She also told me that she had a friend who lived in Pennsylvania, not far from Clarks-Summit, and gave me her phone number. Of course, I followed up on it. I don't recall her name, but I'll call her Angel. It turned out that she was part of a music ministry in her church and offered not only to pray for John but to visit him as well. There was a lot of snow at that time, so my husband and I had decided that it wouldn't be a good idea for us to make the long trip to visit John at the hospital. Also I thought that it would be too emotional for me to see him in that setting, so we were very grateful that Angel would be visiting him. She telephoned me after her visit with John and said that she went there with another person from her ministry. They both brought their guitars, played them and sang with John, and then prayed with him. Angel also told me that John was very receptive to them and that they would go back again in a few days if he was still there. It turns out that my initial phone call to my friend started a chain reaction. She called some people with my prayer request, and they called other people and so on. I don't know how many people were praying for John, but I knew that God would hear their prayers.

The third thought that came to me was to contact a priest in Clarks-Summit and ask him to visit John, bring him communion, and pray with him. Much to my surprise, the priest refused my request. I don't know where I got the courage from, probably because I was really upset at his refusal, but I asked him, "Would Jesus say no?" I reminded him of his commitment as a priest to follow the ways of Jesus. After a moment of silence, Father humbly apologized, said I was right, and that he would go to visit John. After his visit, Father telephoned me, said that he was glad he went, and that John was receptive to his visit. Of course, I thanked him very much. Personally I think he had never been to a psychiatric hospital before and that he was uncomfortable with having to go there. God certainly acts in mysterious ways, doesn't He?

John was released from the hospital five days later on February 20 and returned to Keystone. I never received any further information either from the hospital or from Keystone and unfortunately at the time, neither my husband or I had the presence of mind to request a follow-up report. However, when I decided to write this book, I contacted both Keystone and Clarks-Summit Hospital in hopes that they could provide me with information pertaining to the incident but because of the many years between then and now, we were told that the records were no longer available.

CHAPTER
56

About two weeks later, we received a copy of a letter which was sent to Mr. Frank Nappa, a case worker at the Department of Mental Retardation in Trenton, New Jersey. Attached was John's evaluation dated 1/17/79. In the letter, Mrs. Lozzi stated that "The report showed that John was exhibiting several areas of regression and it was obvious that upon his graduation from Keystone in the spring, they would not have a situation suitable to his needs." She requested that he speak with Mr. Bella from the Fair Lawn School District and possibly consider alternate placement.

We were under the impression that things were going well for John, but this letter and latest evaluation was not only unexpected but gave us a totally opposite picture as to what was going on in John's life. The evaluation was four pages long and quite detailed, so I'm presenting only a summary of its contents.

First of all, it read that John had very little association with his peers and was usually oblivious to their presence which was completely different from John's letter to us only two weeks earlier. The report also stated that John did not get along with others and that:

> His self-interest prevents him from participating in activities such as dances, movies, birthday parties, carnivals, musical activities, arts and crafts, trips in to the community for pizza, visits to the lake in the summer, or other social or recreational activities.

This too was opposite to what we were told earlier. Secondly:

> John is quite careless about his appearance. He makes no effort to bathe or brush his teeth unless pressured to do so. He makes no attempt to zipper, tie, or button his clothes. He rocks back and forth until someone helps him. John needs supervision to make his bed, and sometimes takes it apart again two or three times. His table manners are poor. If not watched closely, John will take food from the other resident's plates, and will take the food with his hands rather than with the proper utensils.

Most disturbing to us was that John made frequent, unnecessary trips to the bathroom throughout the day and night and very often, was found stuffing toilet tissue into his rectum. Lastly the evaluation stated that John had become a severe behavior problem within the last six months and had not responded to any form of behavior modification either at school or in residence. He had become quite involved with self-punishment. He constantly chewed on his fingers until they bled. He would not keep his shoes on and would remove his clothing several times after they had been put on him. The report went on to say that recently in school, John had developed a habit of dropping his trousers and running up and down the halls spanking himself. His only response to any direction was a laugh.

> His overall achievement at present is at a standstill. John shows no interest or aptitude for any work-oriented situation. He rejects instruction and will not focus on the subject or the individual attempting to instruct him.

When all was said and done, John was categorized as severely retarded in his intellectual and social development. One can't possibly imagine the devastating emotions we experienced reading this report which came to us from out of the blue, following the positive letter we had received from John only two weeks earlier. If all of this started six months ago, how come we were never informed until now? What happened? Something must have triggered this change in John; and even though we questioned it, we were never able to get any more information about it. However, things moved rather quickly within the next two months that followed which we thought was very unusual for the state. Nevertheless, there was correspondence among Ms. Lozzi, Mr. Nappa, and Mr. Bella who were making plans for John to be transferred to a different facility. I never received any written correspondence from them regarding their discussions. However, Mr. Bella telephoned us to inform us of what was to take place.

The final result from their discussions came to us by letter from the State of New Jersey, Department of Human Services in Trenton, New Jersey, notifying us that our son would be admitted to Woodbine State School in Woodbine, New Jersey, on March 20, 1979, between 9:00 and 11:00 a.m. We were to provide transportation to the facility. A medical examination would be required forty-eight hours prior to admission, and we would need to have a copy of John's birth certificate and immunization record with us as well. They would be sending us additional material directly from the Social Service Department at Woodbine State School. The letter concluded with, "I think both you and John will be happy with the care and program given by the school. Very truly yours, Assistant Chief, Bureau of Field Services."

When my husband and I first made the decision to place John in residential care outside our home, Mr. Bella was the person who took us to see three facilities run by the state. Today these places are run differently than they used to be. Back then, however, we were not very happy with what we saw, and they were definitely not the kind of facility that we would want our son to live in. Now we were faced with John being transferred to Woodbine State School. There were no other openings available, and we had no other choice but to approve the transfer which we did with heavy hearts.

I had a hard time believing that God would allow this to take place in our lives. When I complained to Him and asked what had happened to all of the prayers which were said for John, along with the words from the prophet Habakkuk, the answer came once again from the Holy Bible. This time, it was in the book of Proverbs, chapter 3. "Trust in God with all your heart and lean not on your own understanding." It was pretty clear to us that God knew what He was doing even though we didn't agree with it. We still had to "wait for the vision. It would not be late."

CHAPTER
57

The first correspondence we received from Woodbine State School was dated March 9, 1979, signed by the superintendent and a social worker welcoming us to their facility. It informed us where to bring John for his admission on March 20 and enclosed a seven-page form which we had to fill out, sign, and bring with us. We also received a list of necessary clothing to bring with us as well.

Woodbine State School was located in Woodbine, New Jersey, in Cape May County on 164 acres of land. At the time of John's admission, it housed 1,000 males. It has since become co-ed, and I'm sure that there have been many other changes made since then as well. There were 29 major buildings, 17 of which were referred to as cottages. Each cottage had a dining area, kitchen, dayroom, visitor's lounge, and dormitory-style sleeping arrangements. There was also a large, fenced-in outdoor play-and-exercise area. There was a fully equipped hospital on the premises with 4 25-bedwards which provided for medical and dental services with both an in-patient and out-patient department. The Woodrow Center building contained an auditorium and kitchen area used for church services, recreation, and holiday activities. A commercial snack bar was located in this center for the benefit of residents, employees, and visitors. A galley card could be purchased for the residents' use or to have purchases made for them. There was a picnic area and a playground on the premises as well.

On the day of John's admission, we were met in the administration building by a social worker. After a few minutes of introductions and small talk, we were given a parents' handbook and then taken to the hospital building where John would be admitted for medical clearance. Then he would be assigned to a temporary cottage for evaluation and placement. This had to be completed within thirty days from his admission date. Recommendations would then be made by the Cottage Program Committee and sent to the superintendent for approval. A letter would be sent to us with the information about John's program and the cottage assignment about which we could contact the Social Service Department for further information or discussion.

Each resident was guaranteed to have an annual comprehensive evaluation so that an individual program could be developed in order to allow maximum realization of their potential. A Cottage Program Committee with representation from different departments would outline a specific program for each resident, with both short and long-term goals, and to provide a follow-up on each recommendation. The ultimate goal of the facility was to provide a culturally-enriched, home-like atmosphere, and an opportunity for spiritual development on grounds and in the community. Administration would strive to recruit the most qualified applicants as staff and provide training for them to enable the institution to provide the residents with the highest quality of care obtainable.

Residents would be assigned to cottages by peer groups. Age, adaptive behavior, and physical and mental capabilities would be taken into consideration in making the placement. Corporal punishment was absolutely prohibited. The resident could be restrained or isolated only in emergency situations for the control of violent, disturbed, or repressed behavior which had resulted in or could immediately result in harm to himself, some other person, or substantial property damage. Conditions for restraint or isolation were to be rigidly controlled with checks made and recorded every fifteen minutes.

These are just the highlights of the parent's handbook given to us at the time of John's admission. We had never received anything like this before. There were rules and regulations for just about everything. This was to be a new experience not only for John but for us as well.

CHAPTER
58

Although things didn't look too bad on paper, somehow, I knew that my observations and fears of having John live in a facility run by the state had the possibility of becoming reality. I wasn't entirely wrong!

The first cottage that John was assigned to was number 16. It housed forty males, different ages, and different physical sizes. The only thing that they had in common was that they were each evaluated as being emotionally and socially maladjusted. The cottage was set up dormitory-style with twenty residents on each side of a large middle section. They had their own dining area where they were served in two groups of twenty. The food was brought in on food carts from the main dining room. The cottage was located in the rear of the facility with a fenced-in area for outdoor exercise and recreation and a space indoors for the same thing. The residents were separated into five groups with eight in each group and one person supervising them.

Can you possibly imagine what it must have been like having only one person supervising eight residents in this particular cottage especially when they were all together which would then make it a ratio of forty residents with only five supervisors? It definitely wasn't a home-like atmosphere, and it was absolutely not like Algonquin or Keystone. I wasted no time in contacting the Social Service Department in order to express my concerns and asked for a meeting so that we could discuss the situation further.

A meeting was set up with Mrs. Peddington, a social worker. Before meeting with her, we went to cottage 16 to visit with John. The cottage was very plain with nothing to look at but the walls. Some of the residents, including John, were outside but whether inside or outside, they were either walking around, pacing back and forth, or just sitting around doing nothing. Some were talking to themselves both quietly or loudly, and many seemed agitated. The supervisors were trying to keep the residents under control. It was not a pretty sight. One of the supervisors, who obviously knew that we were coming, brought John over to us. We were happy to see each other, but I could hardly wait to get him and us out of there. We went to the galley, got some snacks, and brought them out to one of the picnic areas where we spent time with John until the scheduled meeting with Mrs. Peddington.

After the usual introductions and small talk, our question to her was, "How did the Cottage Program Committee come up with the recommendation that John should be placed in C-16?" We knew that the report from Ms. Lozzi at Keystone which said that "John was self-abusive, very disruptive, that he began using obscene and pro-fane language, and also that he constantly masturbated at any time, any place" was part of it. However, we also knew that when John was admitted to Woodbine, there was no observance of any of these things. They did note that he picked around his fingernails and quite often, they would bleed, that he occasionally spanked himself, and that his language was foul. As for the foul language, I am convinced that in order for John to be able to verbalize it as well as he did, he must have heard it used by someone quite often. It couldn't have come from out of a clear-blue sky, and he couldn't have made it up. We suspected that John was sexually abused at Keystone but since we had no proof, we didn't pursue it. I was told that there was a resident in John's unit who used vulgar and profane language, so it was no surprise to us that John's use of this language would increase, and it did. The answer to our question as to why John was assigned to C-16 was that after all things were considered, the Cottage Program Committee decided that it would be the best placement for him. We were getting nowhere in our discussion. When we left Woodbine that day, we were determined to get John in to a different cottage. We knew that it wouldn't happen overnight, but this was the beginning of our efforts to make it happen.

It took six months before it came to pass. In those six months, John had three different social workers assigned to him and on three different occasions when we visited him, there was someone new for us to speak to. I'm sure that these changes caused some confusion to John and to other residents as well. Also some of the employees we spoke to about our son's care answered our questions with the words *I don't know* or *The person you need to speak with isn't here right now.* Sometimes it was assumed that we already knew the answer to our questions. However, because of the lack of communication between us and the supervising personnel, we did not know very much about John's care. For instance, most of our visits with John were in the afternoon and if it was a bright, sunny day, we'd take him outside. We were never made aware, however, that because of the medications he was taking, John was not allowed to be out in the sun from 10:00 a.m. to 2:00 p.m., but who knew! So much for well-qualified personnel. Another thing we found out was that John, and others, were not allowed to use a fork to eat with because one of the residents might grab it and use it as a weapon. That was pretty frightening to hear.

CHAPTER

59

I had little correspondence with anyone during the time John spent living in C-16, and I've blocked out my memories of the six months that he was there. All I remember about that time was that I had many nightmares. I would wake up frightened and shaking, and I would cry. My husband had to hold me until I could get back to sleep again. I'm sure that we went to visit John a couple of times and took him out for a few hours, but all that I can say is that time couldn't go by fast enough for him to be transferred to a different cottage.

We finally managed to arrange an appointment in October with Ms. Fragola, the superintendent at Woodbine. She spent quite a bit of time with us when we met, listened to our concerns, and answered our questions. We suggested that they could make the cottage look attractive by painting designs, shapes, and pictures on the walls to bring in some color. We asked them to take advantage of the nice weather and make sure that John got outdoors more often. He looked a little pale to us. This was when we found out that he shouldn't be in the sun between 10:00 a.m. and 2:00 p.m. However, I was pretty sure that on all those acres, a spot without sun could be found where they could take him. We asked if John could take part in the work program around the cottage and help out somehow. We asked that they be sure that John would take part in the Catholic services which were available at Woodbine. We wanted John to have a galley card and someone to take him there for a milkshake every day since he had lost some weight. If there was no one available, then they should have someone bring it to him. We also asked them to make sure that John got his snacks every day. We asked for an update on his medications. We also questioned the qualifications of the employees since some of them weren't able to answer our questions when we called or even use common sense. For instance, John had a scab on his arm which he picked at, and it wasn't able to heal properly. Nobody thought to put a long-sleeve shirt on him in order to cover it.

When all was said and done, Ms. Fragola said that she understood our concerns and that she would take a personal interest in making sure that things would progress in seeking a transfer for John to be assigned to a different cottage. We were pleased with the meeting, thanked her for spending so much of her time with us, and we left for home believing that she would do her best to help make the transfer a reality.

Six months later, we received a phone call with a follow-up letter to inform us that a decision was made and John was being transferred to cottage 2. It had recently been renovated and would also have a fairly low-resident population. Some of the residents would be going out to a Day Training Program which would further reduce the number of residents in the cottage during the day. We were reassured that the environment would be pleasant and that the residents would be a compatible group. Needless to say, we were very pleased with this news and thanked God for the change.

CHAPTER
60

Cottage 2 seemed to be a good change for John. The staff people were working with him in developing his communication, perception, social, and gross motor skills. They were also helping him to improve his personal care such as toothbrushing, bathing, shaving, and dressing. They were trying to get him to participate in various sports and other activities and to assist with simple chores around the cottage. The progress was slow but steady. He was receiving double portions and seconds on the foods he liked and made trips to the galley for snacks and shakes. Obviously he was gaining back the weight he lost plus a little more. His aggressive behavior was still a problem. It was determined that the behavior was a psychological problem, and they were working with John in an effort to overcome the aggression. He was attending Catholic services and receiving Holy Communion. We received letters from John letting us know that he was fine, was attending dances and parties, having fun, and enjoying listening to music. The volunteer who was writing for him would guide his hand and help him to write his name at the end of the letter. At last, John was getting the attention and care that he needed.

There was one incident, however, when he had an accident. We received a letter from Mr. Blanks, Assistant Superintendent. It was reported that John was sitting on a chair in the dayroom when he jumped up, ran to the window, and shoved his left arm through the glass pane. He was taken to the hospital immediately. It required thirteen stitches to close the wounds to his hand and arm. He was returned to the cottage, and thank God he was doing fine. John was under supervision at the time, but he was so fast that it was impossible to stop him. It reminded us of the time when he almost tipped the refrigerator over onto himself.

Unfortunately John remained in cottage 2 for less than two years. After that, John would be transferred from one cottage to another until a satisfactory placement would be made that would suit his needs. So ready, set, here we go!

CHAPTER

61

It was August 1981 when we received a letter from Ms. Fragolli, stating that the Interdisciplinary Team recommended that John be transferred to cottage 17 where a more appropriate peer group and programming could be provided for him. No explanation was given for the transfer. Most likely, it was because of the incident with John's left arm. It was also noted that in one of his evaluations, John was behaving aggressively toward other residents in the cottage.

John would only reside in cottage 17 until July1982. During those eleven months' time, his self-abuse continued, but progress was being made toward reducing this behavior. John's overall aggressiveness was being greatly reduced as well. The staff recognized that John had a poor self-image and that his need for attention was possibly the basic cause for his aggressive behavior toward the residents who were receiving attention. John was not a behavior problem during recreational activities in which he participated on a regular basis. He was enjoying cottage outings to the circus, zoo, picnics, and Great Adventure. Speech therapy was being provided, and he was involved in the volunteer writing program which meant that someone would talk to John and then write a letter to us on John's behalf.

I decided to paint a banner to brighten up John's room. I painted it on a window shade. There was a large daisy going up the middle of the painting with a happy face in the center of the flower. It was brightly colored all around and in large letters, I painted the words "God loves you!" I sent it to the main office, and they turned it over to cottage 17. I received a letter signed by the Superintendent and the Director of Volunteer Services, thanking me for the beautiful banner which would add a home-like atmosphere to John's room.

Everything was moving along quite well. John had made a quick adjustment to his new surroundings. However, in July 1982, we received a letter from the Habilitation Plan Coordinator.

> Dear Mr. and Mrs. Artale: As a result of our renovations program, John was transferred to Cottage 13 on Wednesday, July 14, 1982. At this time, it is undetermined as to whether or not this will be a permanent placement. As changes occur, we will keep you informed.

There would be two more transfers after this one. The banner I painted never got transferred with him. When I questioned it, no one knew where it was. We never saw it again.

CHAPTER
62

John would reside in cottage 13 until November 17. In those four months, not many changes were made. The programs and activities he was involved in were continued. John was responding well to members of the staff and although he still preferred being alone, he was getting along with his peers. John was in the resident-wage program at this point, and he was collecting laundry and helping to fold towels. The wages he earned went in to his account. The consulting psychologist reported that John seemed to be a good candidate for the Intramural Prevocational Program. That was a first! He also noticed that John tended to be jealous when he perceived others closely interacting with staff, so an increased amount of one-on-one interaction between John and staff during structured activities was recommended by him as a way of reducing overall aggressiveness, and it worked. Since his transfer to C-13, reports indicated a very low frequency of behavior problems. John was also doing well in speech therapy. He was able to state his name and correctly identify objects, pictures, body parts, actions, and colors and exhibited good matching abilities. Although John had been able to do these things earlier on, he had stopped for some reason known only to him, and now, he was back on track.

We visited John in July shortly after he was transferred. We had a pleasant visit with him. He looked well and was happy to see us. We took him out to lunch and to the zoo where he enjoyed seeing his favorite animals—the donkeys. We made follow-up phone calls to find out how he was doing and each time, the staff was courteous and answered our questions as well as they could. The best comment we got was, "John is determined to do what he wants to do." We were generally pleased with how things were going for John in C-13. But then, the next letter came. It read the same as all of the others.

> As a result of our renovations program, John was transferred to cottage 10 on November 17, 1982. At this time, it is undetermined as to whether or not this will be a permanent placement. As changes occur we will keep you informed.

At this point, my husband and I were very upset. How much longer were these transfers going to take place? How could John be expected to make progress if he wasn't given time to adjust in one cottage before being transferred to another one? We made an appointment to meet with the superintendent, Mr. Blanks, and we made our complaints to him loud and clear. We expressed our concerns and our anger and told him that these transfers of John from one cottage to another was unacceptable and that a more permanent placement had to be made for him as soon as possible.

It was about this time that we met Ted Scheick from the Social Services Department at Woodbine. He was familiar with John and when we met with Ted, we discussed all of our concerns regarding the many transfers and adjustments which John went through over the past four years. He was very sympathetic to our concerns and said that he would do whatever he could to help us. We had communications with Ted several times after our meeting, informing us of how things were progressing. Finally in June 1983, John was transferred to cottage 5 where he remained for ten years.

Cottage 5 turned out to be a good placement for John. He continued many of the programs he was involved with, and he was making some progress. Although he seemed to get along with his peers, he still preferred being alone and, of course, continued to enjoy special attention from the staff. John was also making progress toward reducing his incidents of bad behavior. However, over the course of ten years residing in cottage 5, it was as though John was on a roller coaster. There were periods of time when he was making progress in all areas and other times when things took a downturn.

In looking over his records for this time span and beyond, I made a discovery. Something I had never noticed before. John was taking medication in order to control seizures and reduce his aggressive behavior. The medications were regularly monitored and over time, changes had to be made. It became a matter of trial and error. When a medication didn't work well, it would be discontinued, reduced, or increased in dosage, or replaced with something else. With each medication, there were side effects. Some of the side effects listed were headache, constipation, dryness of mouth and nose, blurring vision, nervousness, diarrhea, involuntary/repetitive/jerky movements, dizziness, unsteady gait, drooling, sleep problems, anxiety, confusion, aggressive behavior, may increase or decrease blood levels, and lastly, could expose the client to more seizures.

In today's world of medicine, there are probably newer and better medications available for people like John, but I also think that at least some of them are still used for the same needs as his were. Therefore, you can imagine that the side effects from these medications could have had an effect on his problems. In any event, the medications certainly left their mark on John's life.

Things were moving along fairly well. John's aggressive behavior was diminishing. The doctor said that he had not seen John acting aggressively for the past one to two years and that any episodes reported were directed toward himself such as punching himself or picking at his skin.

CHAPTER

63

Around this time, Regina was in her second year of college at the Franciscan University in Steubenville, Ohio, and in one of her classes, they were discussing family history. She telephoned me and asked if I knew anything about her background. I didn't, but I told Regina that I would try to find out what I could. The next day, I put in a call to Catholic Charities. I spoke to a person named Marie who told me that she couldn't give any information to me but that she would give whatever information she had to Regina. Then Marie asked me if I wanted information about John as well. I told her that I didn't need it, but she said that it wasn't going to cost anything, so why not? I told her that there was no way that she could give the information to John because of his disabilities and that he was residing at that time in Woodbine State School. Marie told me that under the circumstances, she would be able to give the information to me, so I thought about it and told her to go ahead with it.

The next time that Regina came home on a break, we made an appointment to meet with Marie at the Catholic Charities office. She was able to tell Regina that her birth mother had passed away two years earlier from breast cancer, that she was baptized in St. Aedan's Church in Jersey City, and that there was no information recorded about her birth father.

The interesting information which she gave us about John was that he had an older brother who was also adopted by a family living in New Jersey. His name is Anthony, and he is living now in Pennsylvania. She offered to contact him to find out whether or not he would be interested in knowing about John and perhaps even meeting him. I didn't think that it was a good idea at the time, so we didn't follow through with it.

When Regina came home on that break, John was also home for a visit with us. When my husband went to pick up Regina at the airport, I was alone with John, listening to music in our family room. Suddenly John got up, stood in front of me, held out his hand, and said, "Wanna dance?" It took me completely by surprise. I got up and danced with him and when the song ended, he walked me back to the couch and sat down again. It took me a few minutes to take in what had just taken place. It was a very special moment for me. When my husband and Regina got back from the airport I told them about it. John didn't acknowledge it at all, so I accepted it as a gift from God to me.

CHAPTER

64

In July 1987, we received a phone call from one of the doctors at Woodbine informing us that John had bitten a client. He wasn't able to tell us where the client was bitten, but he said that the bite was severe and that it was necessary for John to be put in a restraint. Another name for a restraint is a strait jacket. It is put on from the front with an opening in the back. The sleeves are very long which allows for the arms to go crossed over the front, and then the sleeves are secured in the back. While in the restraint, John fell and sustained a cut over his eye and on the forehead. He was taken to the infirmary for treatment and then sent back to the cottage. Since the injury was to his head, the doctor had to call us. The doctor gave us no other information.

We followed up on this incident and spoke to about five different people. The incident took place at night. The person on watch was on his way to the break room when he heard a noise, went back, and found John on the floor. No one actually saw John fall. The fact that John was left alone while in a restraint, which is against the New Jersey state law, was not mentioned in the report. When we questioned this, the answer we got was that they were in a hurry to get John to the infirmary and forgot to include that fact. Another person we spoke to said that the bite was not serious, that the client he bit was all right, and when she looked in on John, he was asleep.

Nursing reports had stressed the need to prevent injury to John because of his seizure disorder. John had not had a seizure recorded for over four to five years. However, there was one recorded in the same month as this incident. Suppose he had a seizure when he was left alone in the restraint? We asked Ted Scheick to look into the incident which he did. He telephoned us and said that no procedures were violated, only bad judgements were made.

We still had questions. To begin with, the report was not fully documented. We wondered how many other reports were not accurately documented. Was there a possible cover up? How about the client who was bitten? Was the skin broken? John was a carrier for Hepatitis B. Was the client treated in any way against it? Was there any verbal abuse? John's language had become very vulgar, much worse than ever before. The answer to these questions was, "We'll look into it."

Three months later, John's evaluation took place. It was noted that he continued to make good progress at decreasing his maladapted behaviors toward himself and others. The goal was to completely eliminate these behaviors. Other goals were to increase independence in self-help skills, to develop skills necessary for placement in a prevocational program, and to increase communication and social interaction with his peers and others. It was also noted that his needs might be better met in a higher-functioning cottage.

The next note that I recorded was in March 1988. John had a seizure resulting in a head injury. A skull X-ray proved negative. It was recorded that the injury was related to a restraint. Why the restraint? How did he fall? Was anyone with him at the time? I have no other information about this incident, just that John was in a restraint, fell, and hit his head.

Things continued moving along and in May 1989, we were informed that John sustained another injury. This time, it resulted in a fracture of the tibia and fibula of his right leg. A full leg cast was applied and remained on him until August which limited his activity. This was followed by physical therapy for one month. He made significant gains and was able to move about without help. It ended well, but I had no report on how it happened to begin with. Was he in a restraint?

It was noted on his evaluation report that the side effects from two of the drugs which John was receiving were related to his self-abusive behavior. They were immediately discontinued. It was about time that someone figured out what I had mentioned earlier regarding the side effects from medication contributing to his problems.

CHAPTER

65

Starting in January 1990, John's behavior once again became more aggressive. Besides self-abuse, he injured two other clients. One he pushed down and bit the other client's finger. The cause of this change was attributed to the discontinuation of the two drugs which John had been taking. We received a report advising us of this change and that a behavior-modification program would be initiated in an attempt to control his behavior without the use of medication. The program would include physical activities such as the use of an exercise bicycle, walking, and structured activities both outside recreation and leisure times. If John went twenty-four hours without becoming aggressive, he would be rewarded with a caffeine-free soda at 4:00 p.m. To reinforce his good behavior, John would receive verbal praise, back pats, and snacks. On the other hand, if he failed to stop being aggressive or if he injured another client, he would be put in a restraint jacket for fifteen minutes. After fifteen minutes, the jacket would be removed and reapplied for another fifteen minutes if the behavior continued or reoccurred.

The psychiatrist was to review John's progress every three months over one year. The program would be viewed successful if John's aggressive behavior decreased to once a month for three consecutive months. The program seemed to have had some success. That summer, we had John home for a visit, and we noticed that he was able to do more for himself, and he seemed less hyper.

Originally part of John's program would include the use of a restraint chair. Similar to the jacket, the client would be put onto the chair for fifteen minutes and removed; and if the behavior didn't improve, the procedure would be reapplied. After the use of this chair, the client would be encouraged to verbalize what he did wrong and then apologize for his behavior. When I asked for a description of the chair, it was described as follows. It is a well-padded, heavy-duty chair with built-in restraints for the arms, legs, and across the body. A visual screen is then placed over the eyes so that the client cannot see, after which time begins when there is no interaction between the client and the person in attendance.

We were told that this procedure was safer for the client than using the jacket restraint when behaving aggressively because sometimes, it was necessary to wrestle with the client in order to get him into the jacket and also because the client couldn't fall out of the chair once he was in it. This didn't make any sense to me because we were also told that if necessary, the client would be put in a restraint jacket in order to get him to the chair.

My reaction to the use of this chair on our son, or on any other client, was one of horror. In my opinion, this tactic was something that a criminal with a sadistic mind would use on a hostage. It must have been a very terrifying experience for any one of the clients especially since they are led to believe that they are left alone. I did not believe that in this situation, the end justified the means, and I couldn't believe that this chair was put into use as a behavior-modification technique.

I contacted the superintendent and told her of our reaction to the use of the chair and that we forbade its use for our son. There had to be another way. That's when the new behavior-modification program was initiated for John without the use of drugs or the restraint chair. I followed my phone call with a letter to the superintendent and sent copies of it to the president of the Society for Retarded Citizens in New Jersey and to the New Jersey State Department of Human Services, expressing our concerns regarding the use of the restraint chair specifically for our son and generally in all of the State Developmental Centers. I received a response from the director of the State Department of Human Services. In the letter, he stated that he fully anticipated that the staff at Woodbine would address all of our concerns and would develop a program using the least restrictive methods. He also stated that their agency had policies and safeguards regarding the use of all mechanical restraints which were never the first choice of treatment. Their use was only approved when it was shown that other less restrictive interventions had failed. We were to contact him if we had any other concerns. By the time we received his letter, John's new program had already been initiated.

CHAPTER

66

August 1991 was a turning point in John's life. We received a letter from the superintendent at Woodbine Developmental Center informing us that the state of New Jersey had allocated money for the purpose of creating alternate living arrangements for the men at Woodbine and throughout the state. Receipt of the letter meant that John was being actively considered for placement in the community. Group homes were one of the living arrangements which would be considered. A Community Integration Plan and an Interdisciplinary Team were developed at Woodbine in order to provide a smooth transition for the clients. The plan was a cooperative effort between the staff at Woodbine, the community services staff, and the agencies who would be taking care of the men in the community setting. The men in community would be receiving the same medical and support services that they would receive in the institution. This was a positive step for John, and we were extremely happy to receive the good news.

In the meantime, the Interdisciplinary Team at Woodbine met and discussed John's capabilities, needs and health, and developed a comprehensive-program plan. He would receive occupational and recreational therapy and attend off-ground activities. In addition, John was included in a variety of appropriate recreational and cottage activities on a regular basis. It was noted that John had achieved his goal to reduce episodes of aggression and was well-behaved during all of these activities. It looked to us as if the prophecy of Habakkuk "The vision still has its time. It will not be late. Wait for it" was beginning to unfold, but it would be another two years before John would actually be transferred to a group home. Originally the transfer was to take place in November 1992. However, the date was pushed back because of delays in making all of the necessary renovations to the house in order to comply with the standards for group homes set up by the state of New Jersey. Doorways had to be a certain width in order to accommodate wheelchairs. A ramp leading up to the front door had to be constructed for the same reason. A fire escape had to be installed in the back of the house leading from the second floor living quarters, and a sprinkler system had to be installed throughout the house which had to be connected to the township water system. Permits were needed for all of the renovations before they were able to make the changes, and that in itself took time. The transfer was finally made on September 23, 1993, almost a year later.

John was being prepared to make the transfer to the group home in November as smooth as possible. The date came and went, and at the same time, a new client was admitted to the cottage. John's bad behavior started acting up again. Who knows? Perhaps it was the only way he knew to communicate his feelings to the staff. Whatever the trigger, John's behavior became hard to control. He wouldn't listen to any effort made by the staff to be redirected. John would take clothes out of his and others' drawers and throw them around. He was pushing and hitting other residents and staff. He was up at night and so aggressive toward his roommate that he had to be taken out of the room and made to sit on a recliner next to the group leader. John's behavior worsened and became a problem to the staff and the clients. A team meeting was set up to try to resolve the situation. The result was that John was placed on a one-on-one relationship between him and a staff member, and he was not permitted to go anywhere unescorted. Their goal was to keep John involved in structured activities all day so that he would sleep at night. Changes were also made to his medication. John adjusted well to the constant supervision, the daily activities, and to the changes in medication and was no longer aggressive toward himself or anyone else.

CHAPTER

67

It was now three months past the original date when John was to be transferred. I wanted to find a way that I could help move things along. I got in touch with the executive director of Developmental Services of New Jersey, the agency responsible for opening the group home where John would be living. We met and had a long discussion. She filled me in on what was happening—or not happening—at the group home, and I told her what was going on with John at Woodbine. After we met, I decided to write a letter to the mayor of Freehold Township, the town in which the group home was located. I expressed to him our concerns and frustration and asked what the reason was for the delays in opening up the group home. I mentioned that I thought there might be some stalling and stonewalling because some of the neighbors were not happy when they found out that a group home would be opening in their neighborhood. I assured the mayor that the six men who would be living there would benefit greatly by living in a group home and now had the opportunity to live a better life after having lived most of their lives in an institutional setting. I reminded him that these men would be supervised 24-7, that they would be out of the house from 9:00 a.m. to 3:00 p.m. five days a week attending a workshop, and that they would be spending the rest of the time learning and developing family-style living skills and enjoying recreational activities. I reassured the Mayor that once the people got to know these men and the staff who would be supervising them, they would find them to be the best neighbors they could have. I wrote that we hoped that things would move along quickly in order for the group home to open its doors to enable these six men to begin their new lives.

Developmental Services decided to set up a meeting in their main office and informed the neighbors surrounding the group home of this meeting. The purpose was to educate them about what a group home was and the way things would be conducted there. It turns out that the neighbors were under the impression that Coachman would be a halfway house and that the occupants could possibly be sex offenders or violent criminals sent there for rehabilitation. The other concern voiced was that the house would not be properly maintained and that the lawn would be overgrown. After the meeting, the neighbors fears and concerns were allayed.

A couple of weeks later, I received a letter from the mayor along with documentation of the cause for delay in opening up the group home. He stated that Developmental Services did not comply with the New Jersey State Building Codes regarding the connection of the water lines to the house and that the work was done without a permit or inspection, so it had to be undone and redone properly. The mayor advised me to contact Developmental Services and to urge them to comply with expedience. He pointed out that Freehold Township prided itself on being a family town and was often referred to as Western Monmouth County's Family Town.

I contacted Developmental Services and spoke with Ms. Rich. One month later, I received a letter from her with an update on the issue at hand. Ms. Rich stated that she had a meeting with the mayor, the township administrator, the acting building official, the field inspector, and the plumbing subcode official. As a result, permits were issued, and the work would be done and completed within seven to fourteen days, followed by inspection. Ms. Rich also stated in her letter that she believed the letter I wrote to the mayor helped them to move through the process with more communication than before.

It was six months later that I received a letter from Ms. Travis, the group home manager. It was an update which read:

> After a long-drawn-out waiting period, we are finally seeing the light at the end of the tunnel. We had our first day visit on August 3rd with the guys who will be living here, and we will be having an overnight visit from September 15th through September 16th. A tentative move-in date has been set for September

23rd. We are all working very hard to make it happen. We thank you for your patience and support.

The next correspondence that I received came from the acting CEO at Woodbine Developmental Center. It read:

> We are writing to advise you that John will be leaving Woodbine for community placement in a group home on September 23rd, 1993. His new address will be:
>
> Developmental Services of N.J.
> 33 Coachman Drive
> Freehold, New Jersey 07728
> If you have any questions, please do not hesitate to call me.

It finally came to pass, the vision did not delay.

CHAPTER
68

Change was always difficult for John, causing him setbacks in his behavior. Moving in to a group home was the biggest change he had to make in over twenty-five years. It took almost two years to make a full adjustment. His whole environment changed from an institution to a private home and from living with a group of forty men to just six. John had his own bedroom, and the bathroom was right across the hall. The kitchen and the dining room were right there. He no longer had to go elsewhere for his meals. There was a large living room which accommodated all of the residents and held a large-screen TV. Also a spare room was available to use for other activities. The backyard was very large and had a patio adjacent to the back of the house, making it easy for the staff and residents to enjoy many picnics and barbecues.

Another new addition to John's everyday living was that he had to attend a program from 8:30 a.m. to 3:00 p.m. five days a week. This meant getting used to more new staff as well as residents from other group homes who were also in attendance there. They were transported to and from program by a minibus or sometimes by van. The routine of getting up in the morning, getting dressed, having breakfast, then getting on a bus, spending the day at program, and then getting on a bus to go back again to Coachman took some getting used to. Of course, there would also be a change in John's doctors. As for us, we were very happy that having John living close by allowed us to be more actively involved in his life once again. From the very beginning, it was the management team and the staff of the group home whose care and concern for the well-being and safety of the residents in their charge which made the transition as smoothly as possible and kept things going through all the years following.

CHAPTER
69

For the first few weeks, John's behavior was difficult to control. He was hitting himself and others, banging on walls, and throwing around objects and furniture. The staff tried to redirect him, keep him active, and find ways for him to relax. Taking walks and warm baths seemed to help calm him. In order to help John express his concerns and wishes without displaying disruptive behavior, an appointment was made for him to see a psychiatrist for evaluation and also to look at the medications he was taking. As a result, the doctor made a couple of changes in John's medication, and this seemed to help him.

Over the next two months, John's adjustment to the group home improved. He wasn't aggressive toward himself or anyone else, and he became much more involved in activities. The staff was able to take him shopping, to movies, the park, the boardwalk, bowling, to visit another group home, to dances at the Knights of Columbus, and he even enjoyed helping the staff with cooking. Another big step for John was that he started to attend program at the Meridian ARC Center. At the center, residents from several group homes came together and participated in various activities such as coloring, drawing, painting, crafts, games, and improving self-help skills.

At home, the staff was also working with John to help him improve his self-help skills. John was in good spirits most of the time and seemed to be happy. He continued to be active, began to interact more with his housemates and staff, and was very helpful around the house.

John with Mom and Dad at Coachman Group Home

CHAPTER

70

In the months that followed, John, as usual, had his mood swings. There were days when he participated in activities both at home and at program and did very well. Then there were days when he was agitated. He would hit himself, bang his head, and punch holes in the walls, throw things around, yell and curse, and even stuff the toilet bowl. At one point, John's behavior became very aggressive and could not be redirected. He had to be sent to the hospital and was admitted to the crisis unit for evaluation. John remained there for a week. As a result, some of his medications were changed from which he experienced some negative side effects. He became lethargic, wasn't eating well, and began losing weight. He developed tremors and was so weak that he could hardly stand without support; and within a month, John was admitted to the hospital once again. This time, he was under the care of a different doctor. He remained there for three weeks. Medications were changed again, and slowly things began to improve. John became more alert, his appetite increased, and he began putting on some weight. With encouragement from the staff, John was able to accomplish some simple tasks and participate in some activities. He even took some short walks. Unfortunately this did not last very long. Despite the staff's encouragement, John went from smiles and looking more relaxed to showing no interest in participating in activities except for some coloring and swimming.

CHAPTER
71

If you recall, back in 1984, I went with Regina to Catholic Charities and we were able to get a little information about her birth family and also that John had a brother who was living in Pennsylvania. We had decided at that time not to try to contact him. However, after that, Regina was able to find out more information about her birth family and eventually met with her uncle, an aunt, her sister and brother and their families. It was a positive reunion and for a while they kept in touch quite often. Little by little, except for one of her brother's children, they drifted apart again. However, we saw that it was good for Regina to have met them, and we decided that maybe the time had come for John to meet his brother.

I contacted Catholic Charities and spoke to Marie, reminding her of her offer to get in touch with Tony. She said that she did remember and that she would go ahead with it if we wanted her to. I said yes, and she agreed to telephone him and tell him about John and ask him if he would be interested in meeting him. As it turned out, Tony said that he would like to meet his brother. However, he was surprised to find out that he also was adopted and was angry that no one in his family ever mentioned it to him. His adoptive parents were both deceased, but he had other relatives including a sister, who was not adopted, and two nieces. Tony gave Marie permission to give us his phone number, and I contacted him. We had a pleasant conversation. I told him that my husband and I were pleased that he wanted to meet John, but that first we wanted to meet him ourselves. I invited Tony to come to our home for dinner. He accepted and I told him that we were looking forward to his visit.

On the day that Tony came for dinner, we were a little nervous; but when I opened the door, I knew right away that it would be all right for John and Tony to meet. He was a clean-cut, handsome young man who greeted us with a delicious cheesecake which he brought for dessert. We had a very pleasant visit with Tony. We told him all about John's disabilities and how hard it was for us to separate from him. We told him about Regina and how it was through her inquiry that we were able to contact him. Tony told us about himself and that he had actually been back and forth to Italy with his parents a few times but was not aware that he was born there. When it was time for him to go, we gave him a hug and made a date for him to come back again for dinner to meet John. We informed the manager at Coachman that we had met John's brother and wanted him and John to meet each other. He thought it was a great idea.

When the day came, my husband picked John up at Coachman rather than have one of the staff bring him to our home. He told John that we were going to eat pasta and meatballs and that he was going to meet someone at our house whose name was Tony. I was just putting the pasta into the boiling water to cook when they got to the house. As usual, John was anxious to eat. I told him that the pasta would be ready soon and that we were waiting for Tony. Then the doorbell rang, John said, "Tony's here. Let's eat!" However, when Tony came in, he had an armful of presents for John, and he said, "Hi, John. These are for you." John gave Tony a great big smile and had a ball ripping the paper off of the presents. There was a soccer ball, a coloring book and crayons, and a couple of other things which I don't remember.

Needless to say, John hit it off well with his brother. I sat them next to each other at the dinner table. Tony took over, telling John to wipe his mouth, not to put so much cheese on his pasta, and to go easy on the soda. It was amazing to see how well John related to Tony. It was as though he knew him. After dinner Tony left, agreeing that he would be back again. We drove John back to Coachman and informed the manager that everything went very well. Unfortunately we never heard from Tony again. I tried to telephone him a few times and sent him a registered letter which was returned. We don't know why or what happened, but for whatever reason, Tony was no longer a part of John's life.

CHAPTER 72

It was around this time that John began attending a new day program at West Monmouth Arc Center which was a little more advanced than Meridian. Once again, John had to make adjustments. He began exhibiting negative behavior toward himself and others, stuffing toilets, yelling, and throwing clothes and other objects around. An appointment was made for John to see his psychiatrist in order to assess his behavior and make recommendations.

In spite of his change in behavior, John still enjoyed our visits with him especially when we took him out to McDonald's for a cheeseburger, fries, and soda. I remember a time when we took a ride before going to eat and my husband said that we were going to stop at a gasoline station in the town of Brick to fill up. When we got there, John looked around and said, "Brick," which was a pleasant surprise for us to hear. I responded, "Yes, John, we're in Brick."

The next surprise we got was when we drove around looking for a McDonald's. It was getting a little late, so we found a Burger King and decided to go there instead. My husband ordered our burgers and when John picked his up, he looked at it, smelled it, put it down and said, "Throw it away!" What a great commercial that would've been for McDonald's! We left and found our way to a McDonald's closer to home.

Although John had a very limited vocabulary, he was able to communicate his needs and feelings. When he wanted to stop or refuse an activity, he would say, "Stop," "No more," "All done," "One more time," or just walk away. John would also laugh, smile, yell, or on occasion, he would cry. He listened when someone was speaking, and he understood more than what people thought. An example of that was when we stopped for gasoline at the station in Brick.

CHAPTER
73

John made progress in his adjustment to the day program at West Monmouth. The manager, Terry, and the staff were very caring and patient with John. They were able to work with him and get him to participate in the daily activities. One of the businesses in the area contracted with the program to send them supplies of plastic utensils and plastic bags. The utensils had to be sorted, put into the bags, make sure that the bag was closed, and then stacked in a box to be returned. John learned how to sort and put the utensils into the bag. The clients were paid a small stipend for their work, and they were praised and made to feel proud of their accomplishments.

Things were no different for John at program than they were at home. He had his good days and bad days, and his moods would change from one minute to another. Terry found a way to help John when he was having a bad day. She would sit next to him, hold his hand, and say, "John, let's pray." It worked and eventually, John even started to repeat a few of the words with her. Terry was a devout Catholic. She asked Anne, a good friend of hers, to bring Holy Communion to the Catholic residents at program once a month which she did. John always got excited when he saw her. He would go to the door and with a big smile, he would say, "Get Jesus." Anne told me that John was always very reverent when he received the host and consumed it, and I was very happy to hear it.

Because John had some health issues, Terry got him a recliner and a blanket. When John didn't feel up to par, she would have him relax in "his chair" with "his blanket" which helped him to feel comfortable. Also John loved to eat potato chips, and Terry always had some on hand whenever he asked for them. She was a good manager, and the staff worked well with her. West Monmouth turned out to be a very good change for John.

CHAPTER
74

Two years after John moved into Coachman group home, my husband and I decided to sell our house in Fair Lawn and move to somewhere closer to Freehold so that we could have more visits with John. We bought a lovely house in an adult retirement community in Jackson, New Jersey, which was located only twenty-five minutes away from Coachman. Once we settled in, we had John come over for dinner. One of the staff brought him over. We met him at the van and told him that this was our home now, "No more Fair Lawn." We escorted him in, and I took him to every room and then out to the backyard. John looked around at everything, then we went back in to the kitchen, sat down, and ate. Of course, the meal was pasta, meatballs, apple pie, and soda. John was happy and when he left, we walked with him back to the van, gave him a hug, and told him that he should come back again soon.

Thanks for a delicious dinner.

At home, the staff continued to work with John to improve his self-help skills by encouraging him to participate more in their activities. John was provided with a personal album which held photos of the activities he enjoyed. He would pick out what he wanted to do such as playing a game, go for a walk, or coloring. They worked on his domestic skills through participating in daily chores such as scraping his plate after dinner and placing the dish, his silverware, and his cup into the dishwasher, emptying the garbage can, and making his bed. The staff also hoped to increase John's awareness to his personal hygiene by teaching him how to wash his body with a soapy washcloth beginning with his face and then praising him for his accomplishments and his clean-looking appearance. They also continued to work on increasing his communication skills by having daily conversations with him and asking him questions like what did he eat for breakfast, lunch, and dinner and what did he do that day?

Another part of the program was to have John speak to us on the telephone. With the help of the staff to dial the number, John would call us once a week. When he heard me say hello, he would answer, "Mommy, pasta."

And I would add, "What else?"

His answer was, "Meatballs, apple pie, soda."

That was the standard meal whenever he came to our home for a visit. He would gobble up at least two dishes' worth and spoon grated cheese all over the top. I would tease him and say, "No more cheese," and he would laugh and put on some more. The staff would rotate who would come with John because they all loved my cooking. So much so that every once in a while, I would make a pot of tomato sauce with meatballs and bring it over to them at Coachman.

Although John's negative behavior would continue to be a problem, the staff would try to keep him busy and redirect him whenever possible by getting him to return to his daily routine and by asking him, "What do you want?" or "What do you need?" When he threw things around, he had to put them back. If he hurt someone, he was told, "We don't hit anyone," and he had to apologize.

Then there were periods of time when John's negative behavior decreased considerably. He was able to stay focused on his tasks, was willing to participate in recreational and social activities, was very helpful with household chores, and worked well on speech therapy. John was able to enjoy going out more. He went to the mall, the park, swimming, dances, and out to eat. At our request, the staff was even working on bringing John to church on Sundays for short periods of time.

CHAPTER
75

John's changes in behavior seemed to be connected to changes in his routine or to changes in his medications most likely due to their side effects. For instance, on one occasion, it was noted that John was somewhat drowsy throughout the day, so his doctor made a change in his medication. This helped John to become more active and alert, but then he would experience more problems with his behavior. These changes would go back and forth until a balance was reached again.

John hadn't had a seizure in quite a while. However, in 1999, he experienced a grand mal (strong) seizure which resulted in fatigue for a period of time and affected his overall health. John's balance was off, and he had trouble standing and even needed assistance to walk. John began to have tremors which got so bad at times that he couldn't hold anything in his hand, making it hard for him to eat or drink without assistance or to participate in chores and activities. He was sent to the hospital for an EEG and an ultrasound of his gallbladder, liver, and pancreas which came back negative. John also had blood tests done. However, the doctors still weren't able to pinpoint the cause for his health problems. One of the doctors involved in his care came up with the possibility that his problems could be related to side effects from medications.

At one point, John was gaining strength, was walking more steadily, and making good progress. He was willing to participate in some activities but at the same time, his negative behaviors were becoming a problem again. He even had another seizure. Medication was changed again, and John was no longer self-abusive, but he had difficulty maintaining his balance and once more needed assistance. By the end of the year, however, John's health improved which enabled him to concentrate and work on completing his goals with very little assistance from the staff.

CHAPTER

76

John's health and good behavior continued improving a great deal into the following year. He participated more in recreational activities to the point of taking the initiative to ask to be involved in the activities he enjoyed. John also got back to doing his daily chores, and the staff added on a new one. He learned to make his bed, putting the sheets and the comforter on the bed and the pillow into the pillowcase. Because John also enjoyed relaxing in his room and listening to music, he was shown how to choose a tape, place it into the cassette player, and push the start button. He was also enjoying more time going out. If he saw someone getting ready to go out, he would get his jacket and be ready to go with them. John kept showing better control over his behavior both at home, at program, and out in the community. His walking was improving, but he would pick the time when he wanted or didn't want to walk. The staff wasn't sure whether it was for real or a play for attention.

Just as before, things began to change. John's behaviors were acting up again, and his medication was increased. This time, his behavior improved, but just as before he started to experience tremors which started and stopped erratically beoming severe at times. John had been enjoying making juice at dinner time but because of the tremors, he needed lots of assistance and sometimes, he couldn't handle it at all. Another side effect caused John to become off balance and unsteady on his feet. Only on the days when he was feeling all right was he able to do things.

Blood work and an MRI were scheduled, and the results were negative. It was suggested that a nutritionist be consulted to make an analysis on John's diet. The staff at home kept a three-day diet record from which the nutritionist made her assessment. She found that

John's overall food intake was good but was low in certain nutrients and recommended that John be placed on a multivitamin and mineral preparation which would cover all of his needs. The nutritionist also noted that several of the medications that John was taking had food and drug interactions which could cause tremors, and one of the medications could cause liver damage with long-term use. This was certainly an eye-opener. The multivitamin was prescribed, but there were no changes made in his medications.

CHAPTER

77

In the years that followed, John's problems with tremors, trouble walking, and lack of balance made it very difficult for him to work on his goals or to participate in any kind of activities. Both the staff at home and at program were very concerned about John's health and did the best that they could to help him. There were many doctor's appointments and some changes in medication which, as before, helped his balance somewhat but would then cause flare-ups in his behavior. There were days when John was in a good mood and was able to cooperate and participate in some activities with help from the staff. Then there were the days when John would bang himself into walls, rip his clothes, and was very agitated.

One of John's doctors took the liberty of listing all of John's medications on a drug-check website and concluded that many of the symptoms John had, such as tremors, lethargy, weakness or poor condition of joints and muscles, and loss of coordination of muscles especially the extremities, were more than likely caused by interactions of the medications. He suggested that John should be seen by a neurologist whom he recommended. An appointment was made with this doctor, and he diagnosed John as having organic brain disorder on the stem of his brain which enabled him to walk, scream, move his body, hit himself, and go through walls. He recommended that the staff discontinue one of John's medication over a period of two weeks.

Feeling good again

As a result of this change, John was doing better. Once again he became more involved with outings and recreational activities and began to work on his goals and household chores. Two new goals were added for John. One was meant to enhance his self-worth and independence by making and packing his own lunch which he enjoyed doing, and the other was to encourage relationships with his peers by going out for lunch with them once a week which also worked out well.

John also did better at program. Once a week, a staff person would take him for an outing in the community and also two times a day, John would do some exercising. However, tremors, weakness in his legs, and poor balance were still creating problems for John and put limits on reaching his goals. He tried hard and all things considered did well, until one day at program John fell as he was turning around to change his direction. He was in a great deal of pain and was immediately taken to the hospital. X-rays showed a fracture in his left leg and a cast was applied. John was admitted to the hospital where he remained for two weeks until a suitable place was found where he could go for rehabilitation. We visited John while he was in the hospital and so did some of the staff and the guys from Coachman.

CHAPTER

78

On the day that he was transferred to the rehab facility, the manager of Coachman went with him, and we followed behind the ambulance. After signing papers and John was admitted, my husband and I accompanied him to his room and stayed with him for quite a while. Once again, John found himself in an unfamiliar place and was confused. We tried to explain to him what it was all about. We also reassured him that people would be taking care of him and helping him to walk again so that he would be able to go back home in a couple of weeks. We left with heavy hearts and promised him that we would be back the next day to see him which we did.

Before we left, I noticed that his room was not clean. There was dust everywhere especially under the bed. The sheets were very worn, and the bathroom could've been cleaner also. I left my husband with John and went to talk to the head of the facility. I told him that what I found in John's room was not acceptable and that it had to be cleaned immediately. He didn't have much to say, but he apologized and had someone sent to clean the room.

John remained in rehab for seven weeks, and it took a few days for him to adjust to his surroundings. We visited him as often as we could, and the staff at Coachman brought the guys one at a time to visit him as well. It wasn't the most updated facility; however, John was receiving physical therapy every day. He also needed to be washed, shaved, dressed, and fed. I seem to remember that the care he received was adequate. The people involved in his care were aware that we would visit John often as were others from Coachman, and I think that it made a difference in the care and assistance he received.

John didn't seem to like it there, but he was always happy to see us. We would get a wheelchair, bring him outside, and we brought cookies and soda for him which he really enjoyed. I can't recall very much about the time that John was at the rehab facility, but I do remember that there was a long hallway and that halfway down the hall, there was an incline. Every time we took John back to his room, we would speed down the incline and he would laugh.

The day finally came when John went back home. Developmental Services authorized a wheelchair with a seat restraint for John's use to get him in and out of the van. When John got home, everyone was happy to see him again, and they celebrated with ice cream and a welcome home cake. A couple of days later, John was taken back to the local hospital for X-rays, and the orthopedic doctor said that the leg healed well, and he removed the cast. John was still experiencing tremors, and his legs were weak, so he still needed lots of assistance to do most everything. Slowly he got back to working on his skills.

It wasn't until two weeks later that John went back to program. Most of the time, he would arrive in a good mood, and the staff would encourage him to participate in their activities and in the work program as he was able. If he wasn't feeling that well, he would ask to sit on his chair and requested his blanket. The staff noticed that on cold, cloudy, or damp days, it was more difficult for John to walk. Leg warmers seemed to help him, and they made sure to buy him some. Being a little unsteady on his feet made him feel agitated, but once again all things considered, he was doing well.

CHAPTER

79

John started out the following year by refusing to participate in most of the activities. There were also times when he refused to walk and instead, he would drop to the floor and scoot from place to place on his backside. The staff would then have to assist him in getting back up again. John reverted to banging himself into and through walls. It was amazing that no matter how many times part of his body actually went through the wall, he never once hit a stud. John kept his guardian angel very, very busy.

Developmental Services sent someone to Coachman to evaluate John because of his existing functional problems. He observed him before and after dinner and reported his greatest concern which was the lack of muscle control in John's arms, causing him the difficulty in holding utensils. He also suspected that it was possible that John might be using this as a means to get attention or to escape from having to do his tasks. It was recommended, however, that the staff simplify the requests being made of John.

In the months that followed, John spent some time in the hospital. The first time, it was because of an infected abscess on his elbow. He was treated with antibiotics, and the wound had to be dressed and redressed each day, so they kept him in the hospital for a week. As usual, we visited John which reassured him that we were aware of where he was.

Three months later, for a second time, John was admitted to the hospital because of an infection in his arm and again, he was kept there for a week. Each time that he returned home, John had difficulty walking and gradually got much better and was able to participate in recreational activities and also get back to working on his self-help skills. For a third time, John was admitted to the hospital.

This time, because of abscesses on his back which had to be drained and removed. He was kept in the hospital for a week, and then a visiting nurse was sent to Coachman every day to redress the wound which healed well. John had a setback in his activities until he was able once again to participate, and when he felt better we had him visit us for dinner. This made him very happy, and he really enjoyed his pasta, meatballs, and apple pie. It took a month before John was able to return to program.

Finally by the end of the year, John was doing much better and was able to get back out in the community. His wounds were healed, he was walking much better, his health was good, and his behavior was under control. John was able to enjoy all of the festivities of Christmas especially tearing open all of his presents including those from us, and from Regina and her family, which now included seven children. Thanks be to God, John ended the year 2004 on a happy note.

CHAPTER
80

The following year, John continued to work hard at achieving his goals such as preparing for his evening routine by retrieving his soap, towels, and night clothes, turning on the bath, selecting the right temperature, and selecting his clothes for the next day, and he was doing well at it. His season pass to Great Adventure in Jackson Township was renewed where he enjoyed seeing shows and riding through the safari area to see the animals. Also it was observed at program that whenever John seemed stressed, saying prayers helped him to relax.

Three new goals were listed for John to work on. They were added in order to maximize his independence and to encourage self-determination. The first was for John to wash his hands and face after every meal without being prompted to do so. The goal was for John to wash independently by doing it whenever he heard, "It's time for dinner," or any other meal.

The second goal was for John to know more about the objects in his surroundings and their function. There would be a list of thirty-six items from which three would be picked each month, and John would learn how to name it and describe its function. For example, the staff could ask John, "What do you need to wash your hands and face?" And John would pick out the soap and name it. The third goal was for the staff to provide John with more of the things he liked and needed and to get him to ask for them vocally. This objective was also meant to increase his independence. John worked hard together with the staff in order to achieve these goals.

That summer, Developmental Services arranged a picnic for all of the group-home residents and their family. It was held at a nearby park, and we met John and the group from Coachman at the picnic. Besides plenty of food and drink, there was music, dancing, and pony rides. Everyone had a great time, and my husband and I enjoyed meeting some residents from the other group homes and their families.

When fall came, John was still experiencing days when his walking was unsteady and days when shakiness was present. There were nights without much sleep, and John was hardly eating. He was moving slowly and sometimes, he even appeared to be in a daze. Many times, he requested a shower and to go to bed right after getting home from program.

Doctors were notified and changes were made in his medications and once they were changed, he started to do better. John began eating well again, sleeping normally, and was no longer walking slowly. When the holidays rolled around, he was able to enjoy the Christmas parties at home and at the VFW. John also, on his own, made a request to eat with us. Of course, that meant as you can guess—pasta, meatballs, and apple pie.

CHAPTER
81

John's progress continued over the next three years both at home and at program. Although he still experienced some days with problems walking and some shakiness, his physical health was good, and he was sleeping and eating well. This enabled John to achieve most of his goals. For instance, at program, he was shown how to dispose of his trash after lunch by placing it into the trash can, and to wipe his area clean with a wet paper towel which the staff provided him with. Praise and encouragement helped John to stay on task and complete it. At home, John learned how to vacuum the floors in the living room and his bedroom. At first, he had trouble plugging and unplugging the machine and turning on the switch; but once John learned how to do it, he did a very good job. If he missed something the first time, he would go back and do it again. There were a few times when he refused, but encouragement from the staff helped him to get it done. John was also working with the staff to create a scrapbook. He did a lot of coloring, drawing, some painting, and picking out pictures from magazines and pasting all of them in his scrapbook. He also cooperated in cleaning up his work area.

John also began to participate more in community outings both at home and at program. He went to the arcade, the movies, a shopping trip, bowling, the mall, the park, and out to eat. His favorite foods were chicken, pizza, peanut butter and jelly, potato chips, and most of all, pasta and meatballs. John visited with us for dinner several times, once being at Thanksgiving when Regina came down from Massachusetts with her family.

Regina's Family. Left to right back, Regina, Esther, Gina, Eric, Jr., Us, Hanah, Eric, Sr. Left to right front, Angel, Noah, Destiny.

Another big event which John attended was our fiftieth-wedding-anniversary celebration in 2006. It was held at a restaurant, and many friends and family were present. We ordered a special meal of pasta and meatballs for John which made him happy. At one point, the couple supplying the music played the song "That's What Friends Are For." My husband and I were dancing it together with John and Regina. It was the only time that it ever happened. Then, little by little, everyone joined in a circle, moving around us and singing the song. There wasn't a dry eye in the place. It was a special moment, a gift from God that I will never forget.

CHAPTER
82

Over a period of time, John had put on quite a bit of weight, and the doctor put him on a regimen of diet and exercise. The staff had to break him from his routine of eating, showering, and then wanting to go to bed immediately following. The staff made sure that John stuck to his diet. However, he didn't like to exercise, mostly because he was lazy and didn't want to, and they found it easier to get John to exercise when he was given some sort of a bribe. For example, if John was told that he could have a drink of juice when he was done, he was more likely to do the exercise. The staff also managed to get John to walk more, do stretching, and kick and play ball in the backyard whenever the weather permitted.

John was given new skills to work on. One was to complete a load of laundry three times a week. It was meant to give him more independence and a sense of accomplishment. It also kept him moving around more. He had to bring his clothes to the washer, load the machine, pour detergent into a cup and then into the machine, and turn the machine on. When it was done, John had to transfer the clothes to the dryer, turn it on, and when the cycle was completed, he had to take the clothes out and with assistance, he had to fold the clothes and put them away. At first it was a real challenge, but eventually John did an excellent job without being prompted and he enjoyed doing it.

The second goal was to take out the trash three times a week. He had to get a new bag out of the closet, put it into the trash can, and stretch it out over the top. At first, John had trouble opening the bag, and there were times when he just dropped the new bag into the can without trying to stretch it out. After the can was filled, he had to take it outside. Eventually he got it all right and did a good job.

John still needed lots of encouragement to exercise but eventually over time, he lost twenty pounds, and everyone involved in his care, both at home and at program, were pleased with his progress. One person commented that John was smart and that when he was in the mood, he would accomplish much.

Unfortunately John developed cellulitis in his left leg which put him in the hospital for five days. This set him back a bit, but he bounced back in time to enjoy the Christmas holiday. John helped make cookies, went to see Santa at the mall, played air hockey, went to McDonald's for a hamburger and fries, and came to dinner at our house. We sent him home with treats and presents to open on Christmas Day.

Two years later, we decided to sell our house in Jackson. We had lived there for thirteen years. The house was bigger than what we really needed, and it was time to start making some changes like new appliances, rugs, and some furnishings. Rather than spending money to buy those things, we decided to look into life-care communities which have three levels of living. It starts with people who are able to live independently which would mean us, and then moves on to the need for assisted living, and lastly, the need for skilled nursing. We went to see a few places and found what we wanted at Harrogate, a life-care community in Lakewood, New Jersey. We moved in to a beautiful, one-bedroom apartment at ground level, right near the parking area leading to our door, and it was just minutes away from Coachman.

The first time that John came to visit us for dinner, we met him at the van, escorted him to our apartment, and explained to him that it was our new place to live. The only thing that he cared about was the kitchen and that pasta, meatballs, and apple pie were on the menu.

CHAPTER
83

In January 2009, we received a letter from Developmental Services informing us that after thirty-seven years of meeting the needs of residents with developmental disabilities, the group homes and their day programs in Lakewood were to be permanently closed as of March 7, 2009. The New Jersey State Department of Developmental Disabilities was not providing DSNJ with adequate funding in order for them to continue their services. This underfunding had created an accumulated deficit of over one million dollars. The letter stated that the DSNJ management team would work together with New Jersey state officials in order to locate an alternate provider and to make as smooth a transition as possible.

We were surprised when we received the letter, and of course, we were very concerned about the future of the residents and staff at Coachman. We telephoned the chief administrative officer at DSNJ with our questions and were reassured that they were already in the process of acquiring a new provider to take over the three group homes in Lakewood.

Within two weeks, we received a letter from Opportunity Knocks Inc., a nonprofit agency, which would be providing the services necessary to continue the daily-living skills training, medical needs, social and behavioral supports, and the fulfillment of individual personal needs at the group homes. Although the official takeover was scheduled for March, they were beginning the transition early in order to make it as successful as possible.

We were aware at the time that there were several repairs needed at Coachman which had not been taken care of. Also that necessary lab work wasn't always followed up on. When Opportunity Knocks took over, the repairs were made, lab work was resumed as ordered, and some changes were made in the staff, keeping those who were best qualified to remain. We were very pleased with the outcome.

CHAPTER
84

Everything was moving along as usual for John. However, in the latter part of the year, John's health started to take a turn for the worse. He was experiencing swelling in his legs, which was severe at times, and causing problems again with walking. Slight wheezing was also noticed. John had unusual fluid retention in his legs and was sent to the hospital for testing. The results of the tests showed a critical low platelet count in his blood and severe liver damage.

John remained in the hospital for a week. A month later he was sent to Lourdes Medical Center For Liver Disease, where the diagnosis "cirrhosis of the liver" was confirmed. The doctor said that a liver transplant would not be a good choice for John because of the follow-up process. There was nothing else that could be done for him. It was recommended that the staff focus on increasing his quality of life as much as possible.

The staff tried to maintain a normal routine for John within his limitations and to keep him calm and happy. Since John's diagnosis of cirrhosis, he needed to be weighed every day and have his temperature taken three times a day in order to monitor any signs of illness which would be detrimental for his health.

It became a challenge for them to get him out of the house, but the staff continued to encourage him. However, even when he agreed to go out, he wanted to go back home shortly after. John preferred to spend time in his room relaxing and listening to music. Undesirable activities were eliminated, and preferred activities were increased. The same recommendations were followed at program until he was no longer able to go. Prayer was always relied on to keep John calm. John had a preference for certain staff workers both at home and at program. He would seek them out in order for them to spend time with him and to work with him on his routine.

Eventually John needed full physical assistance with his hygiene and the use of a shower chair. It also became necessary for John to be monitored at all times of the day and night, so a listening device was acquired for the staff to monitor John's breathing patterns as well as any signs of distress during the night. A backup plan was put in place as well for a staff member to either stay at home with him or to be prepared to take him home whenever necessary. If a new staff member came in to work with John, for a few visits, he would just observe the person working with the other clients and just being around the house. Then the staff person would be paired off with familiar staff and favorable activities until John seemed comfortable with the new person and be able to work together one-on-one.

The staff was to make sure that there was communication between all of John's doctors and to make sure that going to appointments would only be made when absolutely necessary.

CHAPTER 85

At this point, the executive director of Opportunity Knocks could've had John transferred to a hospice facility for his care. Instead he allowed John to end his days at home, in his own bed, with the people who were his family caring for him. It was a great blessing for John and a comfort for us as well, and we will always be grateful to him for allowing this.

As John's health continued to worsen, he was no longer able to eat, but the staff kept him hydrated as much as possible. Morphine had to be given to him as needed because he was always in a great deal of pain, and he spent most all of the day sleeping. We knew that there was nothing more that anyone could do for him physically, but we also knew that the end was near, so we prayed that the Lord would take him soon.

On September 12, 2011, my husband and I were sitting in our living room and praying for John. We both sensed that the Lord was telling us to go and visit him. I telephoned Coachman to let them know that we were coming over. The staff person said that it would be better for us not to see him as he was, but we told him that we were coming anyway.

John was asleep when we got there and remained asleep until we left. We spent about an hour with him. We held his hands, spoke to him, prayed for him, and told him that Jesus was coming to take him home to heaven and that he shouldn't be afraid. We told him that heaven was beautiful, that he would have no more pain, would be able to walk and talk, and be happy. We told him that he would see his grandparents and Josie and Frank and that he would also see us again when we got to heaven.

The song "You Light Up My Life" was what I used to sing to John very often over the years. He even got to know the words and would sometimes sing with me. I don't know how I was able to get through it but before we left, I sang it to him. Then we kissed him, said goodbye, and left. Early the next morning, we received a phone call informing us that John had passed away at 4:00 a.m. The two people that were staying overnight said that they could no longer hear anything coming over the monitor, so they both went in to John's room to check on him, and they saw that he had passed on. We thanked God that we went to see him the day before.

Our reaction was bittersweet. We felt sad but relieved that John's pain was gone and his suffering was ended. The tears would come later. John's passing was a great loss for us, but it was one that we were willing to accept. We were giving back to God the son he had blessed us with. John was a special child who touched many lives in various ways, and he would always remain in our hearts, our memories, and our lives.

Asking God why or wondering, *If only*, or *What if?* is energy wasted. God is the only One who has the answers, and we just have to trust that He knows what's best and that for whatever reason, John's life was the way it had to be.

CHAPTER

86

We saw John for the last time at the D'Elia Funeral Home in Lakewood. I had never seen John before in a dress shirt and a blazer. John didn't like tight clothes, so I was happy to see that the top button on his shirt was left open. He looked so handsome and at peace. At first, we were the only ones there except for Regina and Julie, who became her life partner. Regina was very quiet, sad, and teary-eyed. Soon after, many people came to pay their last respects. There were staff from Meridian and West Monmouth Arc as well as the past and present staff from Coachman. Adrienne, the manager at Coachman, brought the guys with her, and they were so well-behaved and respectful. One of the guys, in his own way, made us know that John was in heaven. Our relatives, friends, and neighbors also came.

I want to share with you some of the comments that were made to us. The first one came from one of the men on staff at Coachman. He said, "Mrs. Artale, because of John, I'm a better person than I used to be. Knowing him has changed my life."

These comments followed:

"Your love and constant presence helped to shape the services that John received and has enhanced his quality of life."

"When I met John, he was a frail little boy with beautiful eyes and a lovely smile. He was a joy to be around."

"John was a cute, little dark-eyed boy when I first saw him. When I saw him next, he seemed so grown up and quiet. He was a kind and gentle soul."

"When John came out of the van in to program, he was all smiles. He liked puzzles, arts and crafts, and music. Sometimes he would dance. His favorite time was lunch. He would do anything for potato chips. I will miss him, and I can still hear him saying, 'More chips please.'"

"Getting out of the van, John would say, 'Program.' After lunch he would ask for, 'Potato chips,' and later on he would say, 'Go home now.' He will be greatly missed."

"When John was getting out of the van, he would grab my hand and say, 'Help me please,' and when I asked him, 'Who is a good boy?' He would answer, 'John's a good boy.' But the best thing I will remember about John is his smile."

"John had his daily routine down pat. From the van to the bathroom, then off to 'his table' and get a 'blue' crayon to 'color.' Then when it was time to go home, he would get his 'coat' and say, 'See ya later.' I will miss his smile, but I know that he's finally at peace."

"I will never forget John's smile; his love for coffee, peanut butter and jelly sandwiches, and potato chips, and how his eyes lit up when we worked on a craft to send to mommy and daddy. When he had a good day, he would pat himself and say, 'John, good boy.' He will always have a place in my heart and I will never forget him."

"John was special to so many people. When he first came to program at West Monmouth, he gave us a run for our money. We got to know what he liked to eat, and joked that John would be happy to live on coffee, peanut butter and jelly sandwiches, and potato chips. John knew his prayers and liked to pray. I know that he's in heaven. I will miss his smile."

"John was a gentle soul. He was loved by many. He enjoyed music and watching Mass on TV every Sunday. John was quite mischievous at times, and when he did something wrong, he would say, 'Sorry,' and put his head on your shoulder and say, 'John angel.' He was such a ham. He was truly an inspiration to all of us who had the pleasure of knowing him. He will be missed dearly, and never be forgotten."

At the end of the day at the funeral home, I noticed that someone had placed a small bag of potato chips right next to John, and we decided to keep it there. Everything was over. The next day, we put John to rest.

My work here is all done.

CHAPTER
87

Letting go was not a new thing for me. There were so many years of goodbyes, and each one took a little piece of my heart and broke it. The first one, when we brought John to the Algonquin school and left him there, was the hardest. Then every time we left him, whether it was Algonquin or any other place, we had to let go again and again. When John came to our home for dinner, there were more goodbyes. At least at those times, we knew that he was going home where people cared for him and loved him. The final goodbye was the easiest for me, because now at last, John would be free from every disability, and every pain. His suffering was over, and a new life would begin. A life of joy, peace, and freedom. My eyes of faith allow me to see beyond this loss, to a time when we will be together again, and I look forward to the joy which will last for all eternity, and there will be no more goodbyes.

It wasn't until three years later when one morning, I awoke feeling very sad and uptight, and I didn't know why. There were things that I wanted to do, but I couldn't focus on anything. I just sat on my lounge chair, told my husband how I was feeling, and that I didn't know what was causing it. With a great deal of love and patience, he made me aware that it was on that date three years earlier when we buried our son. We had visited the cemetery the day before.

With teary eyes, I told him how much I missed John and that I wished I could hear his voice again saying, "Mommy, pasta and meatballs." I started to cry and realized that I had never grieved for John. I was feeling so grateful at the time that by dying, he was set free from his suffering and disabilities that I didn't take the time to grieve over the loss of him. Every time that I thought about him or spoke about him, all I could think of was that John was experiencing true joy and peace in heaven. I took me three years to allow myself to finally acknowledge the loss and to express it. I spent the rest of the day looking at pictures and videos of John and remembering the happy times we spent together with him and the rest of our family. At the end of the day, I felt much better, and I was able to smile again.

If anyone ever asks me whether or not I would do it all over again, my answer will be, "Absolutely, yes."

Safe at home with Jesus.

ABOUT THE AUTHOR

Evelyn Fraterrigo Artale was born and raised in the Bronx, New York. She was a graduate of the Arista Honor Society at Evander Childs High School and received both the Italian and French awards. She held various office jobs and worked several years as a home health aide. Evelyn loved to cook, and her delight was cooking pasta and meatballs for her son. She was involved in a community theater and took part in many musicals, dramas, and comedies. Evelyn was active in church ministries such as preparing children for receiving Holy Communion, as a leader of a prayer group, and various other groups involving spiritual growth and development.

Evelyn currently resides with John, her husband of sixty-three years, in Harrogate, a life-care community in Lakewood, New Jersey. They have a daughter, seven grandchildren, and three great-grandchildren.

CPSIA information can be obtained
at www.ICGtesting.com
Printed in the USA
JSHW011237241119
2535JS00003BA/13